12   849652

LONDON BOROUGH
OF
LEWISHAM
LIBRARY SERVICE

9780900391101

WITH ALL THY MIND
A Philosophy for Living

This book is a timely contribution to the contemporary discussion of the concept of 'God', and it has a special relevance to the question of whether a valid Natural Theology is possible or whether, on the contrary, our approach to God can in no way be related to our approach to the world. The author refuses to take a narrow view of what constitutes God's revelation to man, and he presents a case for belief in God which is based upon wide reading and careful thought.

WITH ALL THY MIND will appeal to educated readers who have no specialised knowledge of philosophy, as it suggests provoking lines of thought which may well be new to them. The author also shows himself fully aware of those difficulties in the approach to Theism which have been urged by certain philosophers, and he takes their thinking into account.

By the same author

COSMIC MECHANICS AND THE ATOM
A New Model

Though earth and man were gone,
And suns and universe ceased to be,
And Thou wert left alone,
Every existence would exist in Thee

Emily Brontë
LAST LINES

With All Thy Mind

A Philosophy for Living

J. R. HALDANE
M.A. LL.B.

GARNSTONE PRESS

First published by
THE GARNSTONE PRESS LIMITED
59 Brompton Road, London S.W.3
in 1968

SBN: 900391 10 3
Printed by The Anchor Press Ltd., Tiptree, Essex

Contents

Gird up now thy loins like a man;
For I will demand of thee, and declare thou unto me.
Where wast thou when I laid the foundations of the Earth?
Declare, if thou hast understanding.
Who determined the measures thereof, if thou knowest?
Or who stretched the line upon it?
Whereupon were the foundations thereof fastened?
Or who laid the corner stone thereof;
When the morning stars sang together,
And all the sons of God shouted for joy?

JOB XXXVIII, 3-7

Preface

A word or two is called for to explain the rather unusual form of this book; it can be regarded as a study in philosophy for, though it is primarily intended for the general reader, I hope it may also make some small contribution to philosophic thought.

My introduction to philosophy came when I studied Moral Philosophy under the inspiring guidance of Sir Henry Jones, and Logic and Metaphysics under Professor Robert Adamson at Glasgow very many years ago. Sir Henry insisted that his chief aim was to induce his students to think for themselves: a little original thought was more valuable than all the knowledge they could acquire from the great philosophers. He certainly created a ferment in my mind; it played havoc with cherished beliefs and left me profoundly disturbed while I groped for new bearings.

My encounter with philosophy at that time was in fact no more than an introduction, because professional subjects claimed more and more of my attention, followed by the practice of my profession; so that for a long time I found little opportunity for further reading in philosophy. The ferment however remained, and my mind was constantly engaged with those ultimate problems which perplex and challenge mankind, and I was seeking in my own mind for solutions which could withstand all the searches and assaults of insistent reason. In this way I gradually built up a system of answers which seemed to satisfy that test. And when at length I retired from active professional life I committed my solutions to paper. Thus this book was written.

In doing this I seemed to myself to be 'starting from scratch', or at least from nothing more of what I had definitely retained from my brief encounter with philosophy than the proposition that all we know is the appearance of things as distinguished from the reality behind the appearance. Apart from that, my thoughts and reasoning on these matters were

vii

purely the exercise of my own mind, pursuing each problem and train of thought to a satisfactory conclusion. No doubt, unknown to myself, much of my thought must have been prompted by parts of the works of the philosophers with whom I had come in contact in the course of my studies and which had lingered half-understood and undigested in my mind. And no doubt I also received stimuli to thought from casual reading.

When later I read more of the work of philosophers throughout the ages, and especially of modern philosophers, I found that what I had written had much in common with both ancient and modern philosophic thought. The question then arose of whether there was enough that was original in my work to make it worth publishing and, if so, whether or not to revise what I had written so as to integrate it with the general stream of philosophic thought, and especially with recent trends, showing where it differed and how it agreed.

I decided that there may be sufficient that is new in it, especially perhaps in the method of approach, that, if I attempted to revise it in that way, my work would lose more in cogency and spontaneity than it would gain in other ways— a matter of special importance for the general reader, for whom, as I have said, the book is primarily intended.

Since I wrote it the Bishop of Woolwich (John A. T. Robinson) in his books *Honest to God* and *The New Reformation?* has explored some of the ground in my book from the point of view of a churchman. I hope I have something to add from the point of view of a thinking layman.

17th November, 1966   J. R. HALDANE

I. Introduction

The object of this book is to help people to achieve the fundamental aims of their being—consciousness, knowledge and happiness. It seeks to propound a philosophy by which to live, based on reason. Its philosophy is centred in the conception of the complete unity, the absolute oneness of all existence, the wholeness of the universe. Important results flow from this conception in every sphere of life and thought. It appears to arise out of the very processes of knowledge and the nature of the universe as we know it. The universe, under this conception, is not viewed as consisting of truly separate or separable entities, or even as separate entities linked together or associated in one way or another. The 'separate' entities in it are viewed as only relatively separate or differentiated, much as the waves in the ocean, which though quite identifiable, individual, entities, are only features of one great unity, the ocean.

This is the main contribution which this book offers to philosophic thought. It has much in common with Hegel's 'Absolute Mind', though it is reached by a different line of reasoning. It differs from Hegel however in that it views All Being as not merely the sum total of all beings but a complete unity, with a oneness which is indivisible, all 'separate' entities within it being only relatively different. This, reversing as it were Hegel's method of approach, seems to lead logically to the propositions which formed the steps by which Hegel reached the conception of Absolute Mind, (see for instance Chapter IX in regard to Free Will), though they are here described under the figure of relativities rather than antinomies.

The conception of the oneness of all existence (or as Hegel would say all 'being') is more on the lines of Kant's 'noumena', but, differing from Kant, this is held to be one of those noumena, impinging on phenomena, which can be known by reason. We thus do not need to invoke a 'practical postulate' or hypothesis of 'God' to resolve the problem of reconciling the 'categorical imperative' with the individual's happiness.

This book is devoted to working out some of the consequences of this conception; but they are not fully worked out, as they should be in a proper philosophical exercise, because the book is directed especially to certain specific problems, mainly the meaning and existence of 'God', the sanction of moral law, and how to live successfully.

Further, I argue that it is the 'ocean', the one great unity embracing everything in all existence, which alone adequately fits the conception of God. And so this book does not seek either to prove or to disprove or to assume the existence of God. From the standpoint which it unfolds such exercises are based on an inadequate conception of God. It does seek to show that the only satisfactory conception of God, the Ultimate Source and Reality of everything, is All Existence—all that ever has been, is now, or ever could be—in one complete, indivisible, Unity. And such a unity necessarily includes all the qualities which we associate with the idea of personality. From this point of view all attempts to prove the existence of God are meaningless. To try to prove the existence of existence is futile. It is the fundamental fact without which nothing can be. 'God', in this view, is just the name which we give to a particular aspect of existence as it presents itself to observation and experience.

That does not mean that God is reduced to the level of a mere object of observation, like the physical world. The physical world indeed does become, in this view, a part of God. It is a way—the main way—in which God expresses, or reveals, Himself to us. All that we can know of God however (by observation and experience) is an infinitesimal part, but a part which points the way to what lies 'beyond', a beyond to which we can set no limits, and which remains unknown and, to us, unknowable and thus a fascinating mystery.

This book tries to show how, in the light of these principles, a fresh understanding is obtained of many human philosophic problems, such as the purpose of life and how to live so as to achieve it, and the source and authority of moral law. Briefly, it shows that one consequence of this view is that we humans must each be regarded as integral parts of the whole of existence, each vitally concerned in the whole and in every part of it, and especially in that part of it which is mankind. It also shows that, however different its conceptions are from conventional statements of the Christian religion, they are far from being inimical to it, and indeed give it valuable support in essentials.

But a note of warning must be sounded here. It must not be supposed that this book purports to offer any final solution of such problems—that it seeks to dogmatise or to solve for ever the riddle of the universe! The human mind is hopelessly incapable of grasping completely these ultimate realities, for the simple reason that it cannot completely experience them. Only Universal Existence can do that. The best that man can achieve is to create in his own imagination pictures or models of what he conceives ultimate reality to be like. And the ultimate realities themselves can never be fitted into any of our theories or conceptions about them. In the last resort all we can say is that one model, one theory, one creed, more adequately depicts ultimate reality than another.

We look out on the seemingly confused puzzle of life and seek a key or a model, that will reduce it to some sort of order. This does not mean that our particular model, when we find one, is the right one and all others wrong. It only means that our model serves to help us to understand it a little more satisfactorily. It is like the imaginary lines of latitude and longitude which we use to help us to systematise our observations and calculations in geography and astronomy. Or like Copernicus discovering a new model for the physical universe which transformed the apparent confusions of its motions into an orderly and easily understood system; or Newton discovering an improved model which still further systematised our conceptions of the physical universe.

Throughout the book brevity and clarity have been sought as far as possible. And so the policy has been followed of avoiding the cluttering of the text with reminders of the tentative nature of its conceptions and conclusions. Accordingly when, for the sake of brevity, its theories and propositions are stated without qualification, as if they were completely valid, it must never be forgotten that they are at best only approximations—only the feeble gropings of one finite human mind after a better understanding of the unknowable things of infinity and eternity.

A similar warning should perhaps be made about anthropomorphic language which will be encountered in many parts of this book, when referring to God. As 'God' in this book is always understood to mean All Existence, it is perhaps hardly necessary to say that such anthropomorphisms are only used for the purpose of brevity—to express roughly, in the shorthand of metaphor, what would otherwise take much space and circumlocution. After all, as I have pointed out, the conception of All Existence includes all the qualities of personality; the justification for such usage is more fully explained in the appropriate place, before any such anthropomorphisms are used.

II. Mind

Our minds play us many curious tricks, but surely none is more subtle or more universal than that by which, absorbed in the crowding interests around us, we overlook the things which are bedded deepest in the fundamentals of life. They are so completely involved in the scheme of our living that we take them for granted. The stupendous miracle, for example, which is involved in the transformation of the contents of an egg into a live chick is a matter to which few of us perhaps ever give a thought. The egg is, for us, just something to eat; the chicken is just the product which it yields if, instead of eating it, we hatch it. As two plus two equals four, so an egg plus hatching equals a chicken. There is nothing more to it than that. That it needs a rule of logic to validate the addition sum, and that it needs a miracle of nature to produce the chicken, are often forgotten. These things belong too deeply to the fundamentals.

And so it is with our being. It is, for each of us, the most fundamental fact of all existence. But it is so fundamental, so completely involved in all our living and in all our thinking, that we habitually overlook it. And yet sages and philosophers throughout the ages, all who seek to know ultimate, bedrock, realities, have sooner or later found themselves confronted by the simple fact that what happens within ourselves, what we experience in our own minds, is the only thing of which any of us has any immediate knowledge.* It is the only thing we know directly, without imperilling knowledge of the validity or accuracy of any process of reasoning, any calculation or deduction. It is, for each of us, the only truly absolute thing,

* To philosophers this, like much that follows, will appear to be an over-simplification; but it does seem to represent a sort of common denominator, either expressed or implied, in most of the solutions of the problems of the nature of knowledge which form so large a part of the literature of philosophy. For the purpose of the theme of this book it does not appear to be necessary to delve deeper into the matter.

the only thing the existence of which we cannot doubt or question. The fact of ourselves, of our own existence, is the prime axiom on which all other knowledge of any kind is built. It is the necessary starting-point of all knowledge and all reasoning.

Everything else that we know, everything that we know about the world outside ourselves, we know only by the processes of our own minds—by reasoning and deduction within our minds from what we are aware of taking place within our minds. Of the physical world outside ourselves—outside our own minds—we know only through our senses, through hearing, sight, scent, touch, and the others. And we know what our senses tell us only by the reactions which they induce within our minds. It is, in fact, only our own minds which draw for us a distinction between ourselves and the outside world.

We are not, of course, launched upon life utterly naked of all knowledge of the world outside ourselves, needing to begin the process of acquiring such knowledge from its very beginnings. Some of the results of this process of reasoning and deduction are handed on from generation to generation in the form of inherited instincts. This equips us for the immediate needs of the situation in which we find ourselves on our first impact with the world, and gives us something to go on with till we have worked things out for ourselves. But we begin the process for ourselves in infancy, if not before birth. We touch things, we look at them, we smell them, we taste them, we experiment with them; we assimilate our experiences and thus build up in our minds a conception of the physical world which is so well established that, before our childhood is far advanced, it has ceased to be a matter of conscious deduction. The reasoning, the power of deduction which has created the conception has been relegated to the subconscious parts of our minds—along with such other lumber as the laboriously acquired knowledge of how to use our hands, how to walk, and how to speak. These things—the world around us, walking, speaking, the use of our hands—are of such urgent importance in the business of living that we overlook the processes by which we achieved our knowledge of them and achieved the ability to use that knowledge. And so the outside world comes to assume the appearance of a self-existent and final reality, entirely independent of us.

So when one embarks on an exploration of the fundamentals of existence it is of prime importance to have a firm grasp of this fact, and to keep it closely and unswervingly in view all the time. Whatever the outside world may be—whatever it may be that sends these impressions to our minds—these impressions are not the final and absolute realities which we so easily tend to assume. Our own being—our own mind and the life which goes on within it—is, for each of us, the more final and absolute reality. It constitutes for us the fundamental thing, in which alone all our knowing exists, and from which all our knowledge of other things is evolved.

That does not mean, of course, that there is any doubt about the existence of the physical world or of the world in general outside ourselves, or that there is any doubt about the validity of the distinction between ourselves and the outside world.* It does not mean that there is any doubt about the reality of these things irrespectively of what we may think or do about them. What it does mean is that all we know about them is the reactions of our own minds to them, and what we can deduce from these reactions. This is what philosophers mean when they say that all that we can perceive is only the appearance of things as contrasted with the reality behind the appearance. That there is something outside ourselves which acts on our minds in a way that produces these reactions is beyond question. We are as directly aware of that fact as we are of the existence of the reactions themselves, because the reactions impose themselves on our minds whether we like it or not. They are not similar to thoughts or ideas—things we invent in our minds. They are thrust upon our consciousness from without. We have no control over them and cannot even influence them appreciably. We can, of course, exercise a measure of control over our use of our senses. We can put our fingers in our ears, we can close our eyes, we can hold our noses, we can go to sleep or suffer a general anaesthetic and shut out the action of all our senses. But when we do allow

* Even Berkeley recognised the distinction between voluntary and involuntary 'ideas', the former being produced by our own minds and the latter by something else—which is all that is required for the point which I make here. And Hume recognised that we experience the distinction, and at least he cast no more doubt on the reality of the one than of the other.

their action to reach our minds we have no control over what they present. We cannot by the mere action of our minds change the world around us. We cannot by the mere exercise of our wills remove mountains. We have no control over the laws of nature.

But here we must pause to note in passing that there is at least one exception to this rule, and one of profound significance. We *can* by the mere exercise of our wills exert a measure of control over these conglomerations of matter which constitute our own physical bodies. We can make them act in a way which they would not by the laws of nature, which they would not but for the exercise of our wills. We can control our own bodies. But there are very definite limits to the ways in which our minds can affect even our own bodies. We cannot, for instance, just by taking thought add one cubit to our stature; and we cannot by any mere exercise of our wills alter the shape of our bones.

And there is also some evidence (to which reference will be made later) that, within very modest limits, we *can* exercise some influence even on matter outside our own bodies merely by the exercise of our wills. And then of course we can effect changes in the physical world through the action of our physical bodies. That indeed is the chief practical preoccupation of our lives. But all these facts only serve to accentuate the essential differences between our inner minds and the outside world.

A further fact which marks for us the difference between our own minds and the outside world is that the reactions between them, which our sense-impressions of it create within our own minds, are equally imposed on the minds of other people and other creatures; that even when there is no-one within reach to receive the impressions they remain there as it were waiting so to impose themselves. The physical world remains there whether or not there is anyone looking at it or thinking of it. The existence of the physical world is indeed, next to the existence of our own being, the most fundamental fact of our experience.

Nor is the physical world the only world outside ourselves. Our own inner beings, of which our minds are part, are things of spirit; there is a whole world of spirit outside ourselves also. There are thoughts that reach our minds from the minds of others by the spoken or the written word, even by the expression on their faces, or they may reach our minds through their creations—their paintings perhaps, or their musical compositions—or perhaps by telepathy. There are thoughts and impulses, aspirations and inspirations which come to our minds as if for no reason. These are as definitely part of the world outside ourselves as the physical world, and for just the same reason—they are not conjured up by our own wills but are imposed on our consciousness.

It is important that all our knowledge, whether of what takes place within our own minds or of the world outside, is within our own minds; the processes by which it has been built up are within our own minds. However complete and intricate and scientific our knowledge of the outside world may be we must not allow it to beguile us into the idea that we know it best of all, that our knowledge of it is the best knowledge we have of anything. It is all only derived from our knowledge of our own beings and minds, and is purely relative to them. The thing we know best is our own being. It is the only knowledge we have immediately and absolutely.

No doubt the mind is a complex affair, and the more we try to identify our true selves the more they seem to elude us. Even with all the aid which the science of psychology can afford, it is difficult to know just where 'I' end and the outside world begins. But that there *is* an 'I', the 'I' which is aware of all these things, and is at this very moment thinking about them— even when it is only the 'I' which is seeking to identify itself— is for each of us the most fundamental fact of all experience.

It is so fundamental that even Hume, the arch sceptic (as has often been pointed out, and as he himself recognised), had tacitly to admit it as part of his very process of under-mining its reality—the reality of mind and self. If there were nothing for the "heap of perceptions" to act upon, if the perceptions were just like recordings carried on a sheet of (imaginary but really non-existent) dead paper, then however often the perceptions were repeated, the 'carrier' (being dead like a sheet of paper) could never acquire a 'habit' or 'expect' anything. The fact that the habit and the expectation do (according to Hume) develop shows that he was tacitly assuming that there is a carrier and that the carrier is some-thing which reacts to the perceptions—a mind, a self.

But, apart from this apparent self-contradiction, Hume's

destructive analysis of the conception of 'cause' (and along with it the conception of 'mind' and 'self') seems to take insufficient account of the element of will. You have to go a stage farther back in the chain of events than the sequence of effort and 'idea' to find where the notion of 'cause' arises. It is not the mere effort that distinguishes voluntary 'ideas' and acts from involuntary 'ideas' and so makes the voluntary ones seem to be 'caused' by the effort. Efforts themselves are subject to a similar division between voluntary and involuntary. Straining of the heart or lungs, for instance, may be experienced as a purely involuntary effort with a physical 'cause'; and any 'idea' associated with or 'caused' by such an effort is an involuntary one. But in the case of a voluntary 'idea' the position is different. The effort itself is voluntary. It is no doubt experienced as a sense-impression or 'idea', but it is experienced as an 'idea' *and something more*. It is experienced as involving an act of will. We 'make' an effort, an effort of will. The effort and the act of will are experienced as inextricable parts of one complex experience. In this it is similar to cause and effect; but it is not cause and effect in this case because cause is a relation between two events perceived as sense-impressions or 'ideas', and an act of will is not a sense-impression or 'idea'. So the event (the effort) in this case has no other event to 'cause' it. It is in a different category of sense-impressions. It is a beginning, a creation, without 'cause', outside the endless chain of 'cause and effect'. It has no 'cause' unless my will can be regarded as a 'cause'. Including the element of will, the effort may pass into memory and there become a perception, an 'idea' in some mind. But, like 'ideas' (or sense-impressions), the effort including the element of will, is part of the experience which constitutes 'me', a 'self', something existing but not caused, something distinct and unique in experience.

Indeed Hume's analysis seems to take insufficient account of other things besides will. When we turn our eyes inward to seek the mind, we encounter much besides a 'heap of perceptions', including Kant's *a priori* concepts or intuitions, thought (constantly revolving around one pivot or another including the 'heap of perceptions' and such things as this very problem we are now considering), emotions, and will (the driving force of it all). It is true that when we try to distinguish between the mind (my 'self') and these things—to think of the mind without these things—the mind evaporates, it becomes empty and meaningless; but it is equally true that if we try to think of these things without the mind *they* disintegrate (as indeed Hume's attempt to do so demonstrates). They are all, in fact, including mind, interdependent and they are each meaningless without some at least of the others.

More recently, Bertrand Russell put forward the same idea as Hume's "heap of perceptions" in a slightly different form. He enunciated the proposition that the self is not an entity over and above the psychic states or contents which it experiences, but simply the whole set of these states, as unified by the workings of memory and other such patterns formulated by the laws of psychology. It is to be observed that in this Russell, like Hume, is driven tacitly to assume that there is a definite something that 'has' the experiences, something that has a memory and is equipped with machinery or processes which work on memory, and other such patterns according to definite laws (the laws of psychology), in other words a 'self'. But his proposition ignores the prior question —what is experience? The fact is that an experience involves both a something of that sort, a subject, to have the experience (which we call a 'self') and a something other than the self (an object) which acts on the self. Without the object there is no experience—there is nothing to experience; without the subject (or self) for the object to act on, there is equally no experience. An experience consists in the interaction between subject (or self) and object. So to say that the self cannot be experienced because there would have to be another self to 'have' that experience does not make sense. It would be equally true (or false) to say that we cannot experience an object. We experience our self in the same way and in the same moment as we experience (or observe) the object—in the very act of experiencing.

My knowledge of myself, of my own existence, of my own being, of my own mind, is the only knowledge I have which is not derived from anything else, which is direct and immediate. It is the root from which all other knowledge stems. So when we set out to investigate what we can of ultimate reality, when we seek to solve the riddle of the universe, we must keep that elusive but basic fact clearly before us.

III. Matter

Sages and philosophers throughout the ages have pondered and wrestled with the problem of the nature of ultimate reality. What is existence? How did it come to be? Why should it continue to be? Why should there not be—why should there not always have been—just absolute non-existence and nothingness? What is our place in it all? Inextricably entangled in such problems is the question—what is the real nature of matter? Because all we can know directly about the subject—since all we know is by observation—is the reactions which matter creates in our minds through our sense organs, what kind of thing is it which causes these reactions? What is the reality behind the appearance of things?

These are questions which are full of interest for minds which are attuned to such thoughts; but it is no part of this book to trace the history of philosophy or to try to present an account of its conclusions. There is however one point to be made. It is simple but of profound importance. It is this; there can be no interaction between things which are *fundamentally* different. One thing cannot cause a reaction in another unless they have some quality in common. They must each have something to 'catch hold of' in the other. They must have some common denominator.* The finest poem cannot stir a lump of iron ore. Music cannot quell a raging fire.

* Hume's analysis of the conception of 'cause' results in a re-statement of the matter in a way which omits the implication of action by one thing on another, and substitutes the implication of action by a third thing on both of them—an 'invariable rule' in terms of which one particular event must always follow another particular event. That makes little difference for the point under discussion (the similarity of mind and matter). It only makes the test of similarity indirect instead of direct; since the something (the thing that operates the rule) which acts upon both would need to be of the same nature as both before it could act on them. Kant elucidated the nature of 'cause' still further by making it one of his *a priori* 'concepts' or 'categories'. For the purpose of the point which is being dealt with here however it is immaterial, whether we interpret the matter in terms of cause, or of invariable sequence, or of intuition (Kant).

And so that thing, whatever it is, which causes those reactions in our minds by which we observe what we call matter, must be essentially of the same nature as our own minds. Its influence otherwise would pass right through our minds as though it just was not there, without leaving a trace. We would remain completely unaware of the existence of the physical world.*

On the other hand our minds could exercise no control over our physical bodies if mind and matter were not essentially of the same stuff. We could not make our bodies obey the behests of our wills—surely the most striking instance of all of interaction between mind and matter—if mind and matter were not essentially of the same nature. The side of beef which hangs in the butcher's shop was a day ago part of an ardently living beast. Deprived of a mind—even the mind of an animal—and a will to animate it, it now hangs there as a lump of ordinary matter. Or the leg on which you walk and run and dance at the mere call of your will—if it were parted from your will by the surgeon's knife it would become a piece of dead matter, just like any other inanimate object. Your will could not so influence the physical matter which composes your body were it not that mind and matter are essentially of the same nature.

So in essence mind and matter, mind and all the world 'outside' our minds, everything of which our minds can be aware, must be of one stuff. Matter, mind, spirit, all the components of personality, space and time, everything we know, are merely different manifestations, different aspects of the same thing. Their differences are not as absolute as they seem. In the final resort their differences are only relative. They must in the final analysis all be of the same kind of stuff.

So if you would know what is the real, ultimate, nature of matter you need only look into your own mind. Matter is made of the same stuff. In spite of all superficial appearances the physical universe is essentially a spiritual entity.

None of the discoveries of science, nor any of the theories or conceptions of scientists, about the natural world have any

* This is essentially the idealist position, if reached in an unconventional way.

bearing on this subject, for they are all concerned with the facts of observation, with the information received indirectly by our minds through our senses. So, however elaborate or accurate our knowledge about such facts may be, or whatever theories we may evolve about them, it cannot alter the fact that all we do know about them is the reactions of our own minds to our sense-impressions. The 'facts' are just happenings in our own minds.

It is sometimes maintained that science has at least shown us that the whole physical universe is governed by natural laws and that, apart from human beings and other living creatures, there is no sign anywhere throughout the whole physical universe of the operation of mind or spirit. But that is far from being a proper interpretation of what science discloses. So far as science can detect, the human body and brain, the physical structure of all living creatures in which mind is manifested, is, like the living cells of which all living matter consists, just ordinary matter and nothing more. Its fundamental constituents are indistinguishable from those found in other matter. From a scientific point of view, there is consequently no reason to suppose that mind, spirit, life, as we know them, that the living, sentient being which is me—is anything but a manifestation of some of the properties of what we call 'matter'—a manifestation which can be evoked under suitable conditions. There is, so far as observation goes, nowhere else for it to come from. There are no other ingredients in the recipe. The egg which you ate at breakfast could equally, without change of constituents, have been hatched and become an ardently living chicken. And if these properties or qualities of spirit are evoked, if they thus manifest themselves, they must be inherent in the stuff from which they are elicited; they must have been potentially there all along. So that, from the scientific point of view, all the qualities of spirit, including those of mind and life, are apparently inherent in 'matter', even when they are latent.

This is far from solving the problems as to the fundamental relation between mind and matter—between the observer and the thing observed, between mind and the thing which creates sense-impressions on the mind. Science only deals with the thing observed. It does not solve the problem, for instance, of whether mind is limited to the natural world of observation or whether it is something more comprehensive. But it does mean that science shows that there is no reason to suppose that this thing that I am is made of any different kind of stuff than the rest of the physical universe, or —which is the same thing—that the rest of the physical universe is made of any different stuff than this spiritual being which is me.

One may say that that is all very well but one's own feelings tell one that one is quite a different order of being from mere matter. You may say that what I feel myself to be, inside myself—what I feel my own mind and spirit to be—is quite different from ordinary matter. The force of this argument is rather weakened, however, when we reflect that all the qualities which we ascribe to matter (such as solidity, mass, energy, inertia, size, duration, and even the conception of cause and effect) are derived from things which we experience in our own minds. We ascribe them to matter by analogy from qualities which they appear to resemble in ourselves—in our own experience of ourselves—just because they are indeed what we feel ourselves to be.

Modern scientific investigations into the structure and composition of the atom however—the now universally accepted electromagnetic theory of matter—appear to dispose finally of this argument. Matter proves to be little if anything more than electricity in various forms—electric charges of various kinds in groups and combinations, separated from each other at such relatively vast distances as are the stars in the heavens. Moreover in the final analysis science cannot say of what electricity itself is composed except that it consists essentially of waves, of rhythmic variations; that it is these waves which act on our brain-structure to make us observe material things through our senses. So that we can no longer say that what we feel ourselves to be is any different from what 'matter' appears to be—appears to be to full and accurate scientific observation. We cannot say we feel different from what electricity appears to be—different from that potent, intangible, force. It would indeed be nearer the truth to say that it is just what we do feel ourselves to be.

And so the true answer of science is not that we are mere dead matter—that the existence of soul, spirit, mind, life, is mere illusion, as has sometimes been said. It is not merely the fact that it is the 'illusion' itself which is making the investigation, so that it could equally be said to be an illusion that it is an illusion, and language would cease to have any meaning; but the fundamental fact from which we are bound to start, the necessary premise of all our reasoning (the only fact of which we have absolute, direct, knowledge—the experience of ourselves, the minds which deal with these matters) renders any such answer meaningless. The true answer of science is that there is no reason to suppose that the rest of the physical universe, other matter, is any different in its fundamental nature from that little bit of matter, the brain and the body, which each of us observes from within—from within our own minds. There is no reason to suppose that the physical universe is not a spiritual entity made of the same stuff as ourselves.

And so we come back to the conclusion which we had reached already from an investigation of the fundamental facts of the relation between mind and matter—an investigation which is not restricted to negatives. It shows that the physical universe, that matter, must be of the same stuff as the mind which is able to observe it. The illusion is not that we are spirit; it is rather that matter is dead—that there are two different things, mind and matter. 'There are more things in heaven and earth . . . than are dreamt of in your philosophy.' The great universe in which we are such infinitesimal, puny, beings, and which can seem so alien and unheeding and soulless, such blind mechanism, must in truth, in whatever guise it may appear and however differently embodied, be living spirit like ourselves with all the qualities of mind and spirit which we ourselves possess.

What then of the lump of iron ore of our earlier illustration? That illustration served to illuminate a point; but it is only relatively true, not absolutely. The reason why the iron ore shows no reaction to the poem is just that it is not placed in such a setting, and its component matter is not so arranged, as to manifest by itself any reaction to that particular kind of stimulus. Even a brain-cell by itself is in the same position. It takes the complete human organism to respond to such a stimulus. It depends on the setting in which you place the brain-cell. As a separate piece of matter, even as a separate organism, separated from the body, the brain-cell shows no reaction to the poem. In its setting as a part of a human being it does react to it. Similar considerations apply to the music and the fire of the other illustration.

If it should seem odd that the physical universe, apart from living creatures on the Earth, should appear so dead, should show no sign of life let alone of mind, it is only necessary to pause and reflect that the living human brain would look much the same if it could be examined under an electron microscope, or some such instrument, which discloses the individual electrons of the atoms which constitute the brain substance. The electrons would appear as cold, aloof, meaningless dead matter, part of some ruthless machinery making constellations revolve in their set orbits, much like what we see with the naked eye when we survey the starry heavens on a clear night.

Who knows but that if we were able to see the physical universe in all its settings it too would become a significant part of some organic manifestation of life. The whole physical universe as we know it might be something akin to a ganglion or nerve-cell in the brain of some vast being; and all that we see taking place in the physical universe, guided apparently by mere blind mechanism devoid of intelligence—even the evolution of worlds and of living species—might be part of a process of trying out some 'idea' in the 'mind' of that being, for whom of course time would have a vastly different value than it has for us. It may be that 'matter' is just existence (of the nature of mind) which has become comparatively dead, comparatively static in its condition and fixed in its ways—existence which has comparatively ceased to change or develop—ceased to live.

In the light of our present knowledge of the atomic and chemical structure of physical matter indeed, and of the structure and behaviour of the atom, it is not difficult to conceive how any part of the universe we know is potentially capable of becoming like any other part. A few changes in the arrangement of atoms, a few changes in the number or position of the electrons and other particles composing an atom, and all the changes could be rung from the lightest vapour to the most solid matter, from the deadest of dead matter to the most vital of living beings, from the solid earth to Adam, from a mountain ash to a Winston Churchill.

IV. God

From a recognition of the essential sameness of mind and all of which mind could be aware it is a short step to the recognition of their essential unity—the essential unity of all existence.

(1)

It is inconceivable that things which are made of the same kind of stuff should have different ultimate sources of origin or causes of being. It is inconceivable that somehow, out of the void of absolute nothingness, something should have stirred and should have evolved itself into the kind of stuff of which existence is constituted; and that something else should also have stirred out of the same void and should have evolved itself into the identical kind of stuff; or that, however existence as distinct from infinite and eternal nothingness came to be, the same thing occurred more than once, and to precisely the same effect—and that there should yet be no connection whatever between such occurrences—no common cause. And if this is to be taken as having occurred not twice but countless millions of millions of times, so as to include every particle of matter, every mind and every person, everyone and every separate thing which exists in all the universe, past, present and future, all made of the same kind of stuff, it becomes infinitely inconceivable. There is no room here—absolutely no room—for the operation of mere chance. It is a case of the same thing happening over and over again ad infinitum and nothing different ever happening at all.

No doubt it is also inconceivable to our minds, on the one hand, how anything could come into being at all out of the void of absolute nothingness, or, on the other hand, how anything could exist without having come into being. It is inconceivable how anything could exist for ever and ever without beginning or ending. It is inconceivable why there should be any existence at all, why we or anything else should exist, instead of utter nothingness and non-existence. Probably all such concepts are meaningless in ultimate reality. They are beyond our comprehension. Our minds are completely out of their depth in such speculations, groping and floundering in the dark without bearings. But however it is that things have come to exist they do exist; and if we are to think of them at all we must apply the forms which thought uses in its processes. And when we do so it seems clear that if there is a sameness in things they must inevitably have come from the same ultimate mould. They must have a common origin or cause of being. Our whole universe must have a single ultimate source of origin.

And this is no less true of the universe as it is today than of the universe as it may have been in the dim and distant past, and no less true of the fact of its continuing to exist than of the fact of its existence at any one moment. Its fundamental sameness all betrays a common origin.

And things which have a common ultimate origin must have had, and for ever retain, a complete unity in that ultimate origin or cause. It is true that in space and time things which once started as a unity may become broken up and separated; but space and time are needed for the constitution of such a disunity; and space and time have no bearing on this matter. Space and time are not something outside of the rest of existence, something existing independently, in their own right, something absolute, to which other existences must conform. To regard them so would only postpone the issue, for what we are considering is the nature and origin of existence as distinct from the void of utter non-existence; and space and time do exist; so the question would remain in regard to them as in regard to anything else—how did they come to exist? Sooner or later we would have to consider their origin like the origin of anything else. They are just ingredients or qualities in the make-up of that world which our minds make us aware of. And so in the final analysis they must be constituted of the same stuff as our minds and as everything else of which we are aware, and must have the same common origin. Space and time contribute neither more nor less to the solution of the problem than any of the myriad other entities which exist in our world. So disunities which need space and time for their creation can be relative only to space and time and have no ultimate reality.

Kant's analysis of the way in which space and time enter into the world of sense-impressions goes into more detail than this and establishes the point more elegantly and conclusively. It may be noted that his theory of space and time, although in accord with the view stated here, is in marked contrast to that almost universally entertained by physical scientists, as represented by Newton, Minkowski, and Einstein. For Kant, space and time are 'intuitions', which, like abstract ideas, have no content or physical existence apart from the material entities which occupy them. For Newton, Minkowski, and Einstein they have a physical existence of their own quite apart from the physical bodies or events which occupy them, although this was not perhaps expressed, or even fully realised, but only tacitly assumed. For all of them, space—to confine attention meantime to space—is the reference-frame for absolute position, motion, and geometrical formation, and also for all the phenomena of inertia, the frame in relation to which bodies remain at rest or, if moving, their line of motion is straight and its speed uniform. In other words, in terms of cause and effect which is fundamental to physics, space controls all physical bodies and makes them conform to its own position, motion, and geometry and the laws of inertia. For Einstein, space is in addition the frame in reference to which light travels in a straight line and at a constant velocity (186,282 miles *per sec.*)—in other words it controls the direction and speed of light. This leads to difficulties in locating the reference-frame ('absolute space') and also, in Einstein's case, to difficult conceptions about the 'bending' of space in all directions—in both cases in order to furnish a theoretical explanation of certain observed physical phenomena. Time, of course, also enters into these problems, and time is treated in a similar way, which it is unnecessary to elaborate here, so that the problem becomes one of the 'space-time continuum'. In Einstein's case the difficulties are increased by the paradox that while these physical properties are ascribed to space and time the property of unobservability is also ascribed to them. In both cases it may be noted that if the physical conception of space and time be dropped and Kant's conception of them (as having no physical content—empty space and empty time) be adopted, and attention confined to observable and observed phenomena, physical solutions seem to emerge from these problems and others as well. (See for instance, pp. 24 and 25 in *Cosmic Mechanics and the Atom*, 1965, by the present author; and *A Basis for a Unified Field Theory*, 'Amateur Scientist', Feb. 1966.)

The whole universe, including space and time, must be united in its common origin, and remain for ever united, and be immutably One.

(2)

This fundamental unity or continuity underlying all separateness is reflected, as one might expect, in the make-up of the physical world; and the form in which it appears there may aid the understanding of the way in which it works in the sphere of ultimate reality.

One of the simplest ways of expressing this phenomenon is found in the conception of the ether of space—a conception which is somewhat out of fashion at the moment, because Einstein's 'special' theory of relativity would render it unnecessary. The ether was conceived as being a single, continuous, indivisible medium filling all space—the medium which transmits light and other radiations through space—and as not only permeating all matter but as being the substance out of which in the final analysis all matter is constituted. Each piece of matter is a feature of the ether much as a knot is a feature of a piece of string.

Almost the same idea may be expressed in another scientific conception, which emerges from Einstein's 'general' theory of relativity. Every body of matter, every electron and every particle, has attached to it, in this conception, its own inertial field, the counterpart of its gravitational field. This inertial field tends to hold everything else in position relatively to itself. It extends ad infinitum in every direction from the body of matter but in decreasing strength, like its gravitational field. Each field consists of the identical kind of thing (inertial influence with a central core of matter). Together all the fields of all the units of matter in the universe form the medium which both transmits radiations and binds the universe together into a coherent unit (much like the ether). And so the influence of the whole permeates each unit of matter, each particle, however small; and the influence of each particle permeates the whole however faintly. And every movement, every change, in any part has its repercussions, however slight, to the uttermost ends of the universe.

Again, in the physical world, there are space and time which together form that framework in which everything in all the physical universe is enmeshed, and which binds it together in immutable continuity—the space-time continuum. And there are all the other 'laws' of nature (for space and time are only laws of nature) each of which binds either the whole or some part of the physical world in the unity of a common submission to it—including the mere continuance of existence, for nothing could continue to exist from one moment to another unless there were some 'law' which made it do so. And all these laws too are themselves just ingredients in the make-up of the world of which the single mind of each of us makes us aware; and in doing so our mind weaves the ingredients into a common unity.

(3)

There should be noticed here in passing a theory which has sometimes been thought to solve all the problems of existence—the theory that, however enormous may be the odds against it, sooner or later the universe as we know it was bound to happen by the mere operation of the mathematical law of chance or averages. This cannot be done however without assuming the pre-existence of the laws of mathematics and the laws of chance and averages and the pre-existence also of the stuff of which the universe is constituted, for these laws to act upon; and the question would still remain, how did they come into existence? So that if this theory, fantastic as it may seem, should yet prove to have some validity it would only mean that all the laws of nature could in the final analysis be reduced to terms of one simple law—the law of chance or averages. It would only be itself another law of nature—a purely scientific matter of no more concern or significance for the problem we are considering (the origin and nature of existence as such) than quantum theory or the laws of gravitation or the multiplication tables or the instinct which draws the workers to the queen bee. Like all such things it would only be one of the ingredients in the make-up of the world which embraces all existence in one single unity, including our own minds.

(4)

This fundamental continuity underlying all separateness is reflected also in the make-up of our own minds and personalities, our selves. We can analyse them into various faculties and parts, such as reason, emotion, spirit, will, sense-impressions, and each part has subdivisions such as love, hate, fear, well-nigh ad infinitum. And yet my own personality, my self, is a single indivisible whole. We can never isolate any of these parts of our personalities in a completely pure form. Each always has in it traces of all the others. We can never, for instance, experience pure reason. Even a mathematical formula (the purest logic) is invested with associations of one sort or another in the mind of each of us when we contemplate it. And there is no clear-cut division between any of the parts. Even in such an apparently definite case as the difference between sense-impression and reason we cannot really discern where sense-impression ends and the processes of reason by which we assimilate them begins. And none of the parts has any content or meaning without at least some of the others. Fear, for instance, has no meaning without some object, and an object can only reach the mind in the form of a sense-impression. No part of my self has any meaning at all apart from my will—the impetus to live, to realise my self and to express my self. Of what significance could even a sense-impression be except as part of the experience of some living, purposeful, being (man or beast)? The will makes use of all the other parts of the mind, or self, for its own ends; and apart from the uses which the will makes of them they are empty and meaningless. The will, the urge to live, dominates them all; but into however many parts my mind can divide itself, it remains one inextricable unity.

(5)

It is not only what actually exists or has existed that is embraced in this all-pervading unity. For the very same reasons there is included in it everything that might possibly exist, everything of which mind could be aware, everything which could affect any part of the scheme of existence in which we have our being.

It is of course theoretically possible that there might be other existences, of a different order altogether—existences of which our minds could not be aware. But if anything is capable of making its existence known to any mind, whether ours or some other with which ours could communicate, or if anything is capable of affecting in any way any part of the scheme of existence in which we have our being, then it must be of the same order, of the same stuff, as our universe and part of that unity which embraces the whole scheme of our existence. And if anything is not thus capable of making its existence known to us, if anything is of a different order of existence altogether, then it can never, in time or eternity, be of any concern to us. For us it does not exist at all, and so can once and for all be dismissed from our thoughts.

(6)

Reason is a marvellous faculty. It is an instrument designed to enable us to cope with the world in which we live; and its achievements give us constant and ever-new wonder, awe, and delight. But the full content of what is implied in this conception of universal existence is far beyond the grasp of the human mind. It includes of course everything on this Earth, and all the vast physical universe that we know something of, and all that as yet we do not know of it. It includes all the myriad species of life there have ever been on this Earth, all the variations of them which might evolve or emerge, and all the other forms which life might possibly take either here or in any other part of the universe. It includes all the forms which matter assumes and all the infinite variations of it there might be.

And in the domain of the mind and the spirit it includes every person, every personality, there has ever been and everyone there may yet be. It includes all the love and hate, all the joy and sorrow, all the hopes and ideals, all the creative imaginings, all the memories, all the beauty and all the thrills, all that the heart of man has ever felt or could experience.

And since the properties of mind and spirit are, as we have seen, inherent in everything, in every part of existence, they must be inherent properties of universal existence; and all these things as they exist in the heart and mind of man must be nothing compared with the love and hate, the joy and sorrow, the hopes and ideals, the creative urge, all that is in the Universal Heart and Mind. 'Eye hath not seen, nor ear heard, neither have entered the heart of man' all that Universal Existence is or may be. It is without limits either in space or in time, infinity or eternity.* It is a concept for which there is a simple name sanctioned by long usage. So, if only for the sake of brevity, let us call it by its well-worn designation— God.

(7)

This conception of God may be somewhat different from that which is commonly entertained; but it would appear that nothing else will suffice. He could not be anything more. There cannot be anything more than everything that is or could be. And He could not be anything less, for that would involve there being some still higher Universe or Existence to include both God and what is not God in one domain; because, for the reasons we have been considering, since God would be aware of the rest of existence, and because He could influence it, both He and the rest of existence would necessarily be constituted of the same stuff. They would therefore have to have a common source, and be a single undivided unity. And yet God would be only a part of it. He would be subject to its economy or 'natural' laws, as otherwise He could not be aware of it, let alone influence it. In other words 'God' would not really be God, the ultimate source, the omnipotent, the creator and maintainer of all things, the supreme ruler, the infinite and eternal, but only some lesser deity, part of some wider, higher universe or existence, and subject to the governance of that universe. And so we would have to conceive of

* The theme of this book is much in line with Kant's distinction between *noumena* and *phenomena*; but, differing from Kant, it holds that we *can* know a little, if only a very little, of the noumenal by deduction from what we know of its relations with the phenomenal at the point where the noumenal impinges on the phenomenal. (See also Chap. XVIII.)

another God to embrace them both (the deity and the rest of the universe) in one super-universe.

A purely materialistic conception of the universe is inadequate for much the same reason. It does not account for the qualities of mind and spirit which we experience in ourselves, and which for each of us constitute the most fundamental and important fact of existence.

(8)

No doubt this conception of God raises in an acute form some of the problems which have always exercised philosophers and theologians—the problem for instance of the possibility of man possessing freedom of will in an ordered universe, and the problems of the existence of suffering and wrong. These and similar questions will be faced squarely as we proceed; and we will find that this conception has its own solution to offer to them. Meantime let us note that this conception of God involves a consideration of great importance. It shows that our own selves, our own personalities, are not the absolutely separate, individual, beings we are so apt to think. However individual, however separate, we may be it is in ultimate reality only a relative separateness. For we too, with our minds, our spirits, our personalities, are each in ultimate reality parts of this indivisible whole. We have each our lot and part in the universe of all existence. In it 'we live and move and have our being'. We each have a stake in the universe however small our own shareholding may be. This is a truth which involves important consequences for all our thinking, all our living, all our aspirations. It is the truth which expresses itself in such well-known imagery as the 'fatherhood' of God and the 'brotherhood' of man.

(9)

The conception of infinite and eternal, of universal, existence or God is one which it is not easy for the mind to work with because it involves concepts with which we are not familiar in every-day life; and so it is natural and convenient to use figures of speech and thought to represent its import, figures which can easily be visualised and which sufficiently indicate its essential features for ordinary people—figures such as Universal King, Creator, Father, Lord of all. Like all metaphors however there is a limit to the validity of such figures. They are each and all only part of the truth. To take an analogy—when you indulge in day-dreams it is quite true to describe yourself as the creator of your castles in the air; but it is not the whole truth. You are more than their creator. The castles are themselves part of you; they have their existence only in you, in your mind. But they are a very small part of you. You are much more than your dream castles and all the other parts of you put together. And so also the things which God creates are part of Him. They have their existence only in Him—in His mind. God is not only the Creator; He embraces also the things created. But He is infinitely more than that. The whole of creation and of creative activity are but a small part of Universal Existence—a small part of God. And so it is with all such ways of denoting God. They are each and all but a part of the truth. None of them, nor all of them together, can fully depict the infinite and eternal universe of all that is or ever could be, which is God. They are convenient modes of expression for work-a-day purposes; but we must never forget that they only are symbols and metaphors, subject to all the limitations and shortcomings of metaphors and symbols. And so in much of what follows, for the sake of brevity and ease of understanding, God, the Supreme and Universal Being, will be referred to as though He were a mere human being, and it will be taken for granted that the limitations to the validity and aptness of such metaphorical and anthropomorphic language are understood, without constant reminders of it.

(10)

It will be observed that neither this conception of God nor the method by which it has been evolved depend in any way on any of the conceptions or discoveries of science. Science is entirely irrelevant to the matter. It is of no concern for this conception of God, or for the method by which it has been reached, how or when the physical universe came into being. It makes no difference how many thousands of millions of years this world has existed, or whether it and the life on it came into being at a single stroke or by a process of careful evolution, or in a series of cataclysmic happenings, or whether the process of creation goes on all the time—as it does indeed in nature, in the birth and growth of animal and vegetable life, and as it does within our own experience in the spiritual world, as for instance in our imaginings and in the creations of artists, composers, poets, novelists, and in every new personality born into the world. This conception of God is concerned only with the fundamental things without which neither science nor anything else could exist.

The idea that science can have any bearing on the question of the existence of God is due as a rule to one or other of two misconceptions. Sometimes it is due to people becoming so fascinated by the marvels which science discloses that they lose sight of its limitations. And sometimes it is due to a failure to recognise the true nature of the first three chapters of the Book of Genesis. This leads some people to read these chapters as if they were intended to be a scientific account of the origin of the world; and so, by way of a particular conception of how inspiration works, they reach the conclusion that the existence of God stands or falls with the scientific accuracy of the description of creation in Genesis.

Apart from any question about how inspiration works, however, or about the authenticity of 'holy writ' in matters of science, these first chapters of the Book of Genesis no more purport to give a factual account of the origin of the world and of species than *Rule Britannia* purports to give a factual account of the origin of Great Britain, or *Pilgrim's Progress* to be an account of events in history. It was probably handed down from generation to generation by word of mouth and finally committed to writing as a fitting prologue to the Book of Genesis. The real marvel is that, being obviously the work of a poet rather than a scientist, it yet maintains so much harmony with all that science has since revealed about such matters.*

The conception of God put forward here depends on no history, no science, no book or revelation. It is based on more fundamental things. It is based on the fact of existence as such, including the existence of knowledge, of the knower and the thing known, of mind and things apprehended—the things which science and revelation have to assume before they could

* See Chapter XIII.

36

begin. It is an outcome of applying reason in its simplest forms to the basic facts of every-day experience. Science, as the term is understood today, is inherently unable to throw any light on the problems which we have been considering. It restricts itself to observed phenomena, rejecting everything which is not thoroughly established by observation or experience. And so, although it can throw more and more light on the detailed structure and behaviour of the world as it can be observed— on how it works—it can throw no light on what it is that works. The world of observation is composed of our sense-impressions, whether received directly from the object under observation or indirectly by way of instruments; and the some-thing (the ultimate source of our world) which imposes these impressions on our minds, is unobserved and unobservable. The impressions themselves are all that we can observe of it. So science takes nothing to do with it. But it is the whole subject-matter of the philosophic enquiry on which we have been engaged—what is the origin, the ultimate reality, like? How much can we know of it, or can we know anything at all of it?* Astronomy or physics may be able, for instance, to reveal that the physical universe as we know it today has developed from a terrific explosion of a comparatively small body countless millions of years ago; but that brings us no nearer to the solution of our problem. It only high-lights an important event in the history of our universe. What was it that exploded? Where had it come from? What made the natural laws which resulted in the explosion and controlled its form and outcome? How long had all these things existed before the explosion and how did they come to exist? Just the same problems, in fact, as those that confront us by the

* It is difficult to understand why Darwin's discovery of natural selection so impressed philosophers. It deals only with 'the appearance of things' and has no bearing on 'the reality behind the appearance', unless to furnish a rich pool of metaphor to help us in our attempts to construct theories about it. It is not so surprising in the case of Pragmatists and Marxists, since their systems are more of social sciences than philosophies; and Darwin's discoveries suggested that it is futile to look for signs of anything like a guiding mind in the processes of nature. The laws which operate it, when you understand them, have no imperfections in their make-up which have to be glossed over in this way. If there is a guiding mind behind it all it does not betray itself by faulty workmanship in nature.

existence of the universe as we know it today—the problems we have been considering. It would be hard to decide whether science or philosophy is the more important branch of thought. Science today is concerned with every facet of life; but philosophy is concerned with how much it is all worth while, and how to make it more worth while, how to live successfully.

V. Man

When one thinks of the vast physical universe with its enormous stars and myriad galaxies, this little planet of a very minor star, this Earth, seems something less than an insignificant morsel of matter—less than a tiny grain of sand among all the shores of all the oceans. And if one thinks how infinitesimal is a man even on the face of the Earth, and of the countless millions of men there have already been, one feels how utterly insignificant any man must be in the vast scheme of things.

And yet, as Hamlet is made to say, 'What a piece of work is a man! how noble in reason! how infinite in faculty! in form and moving how express and admirable! in action how like an angel! in appearance how like a god! the beauty of the world! the paragon of animals!'

Here is a devastating contrast—two very different aspects of man's significance in the universe! Yet both are reconciled in the conception of the oneness of all existence. For, because of that oneness, everything that exists, however great or however small, expresses something of the whole universe. It is indissolubly one with it. Its individuality, its distinction from the rest of the universe, is only relative. The qualities and features which it displays must be inherent in the whole universe—must be inherent in the stuff of which the universe is made—or they could not emerge in that particular thing, whatever it may be. Everything, however small and insignificant it may appear, holds within itself potentially something of the whole universe. Poets and artists have always been aware of this. The characteristics of the particular thing depend upon whether this or that potential quality of universal existence is more or less developed in it. This is a truth which should present no difficulties to this atomic age. In the physical world it is reflected in the particular arrangement of its component atoms, and in the particular arrangement of the electrons and particles within the atoms.

Everything expresses thus something of universal

existence. That is one end of the matter, as it were. At the other end is the mind of the person observing these things. When we talk of a thing 'expressing' something, as distinct from merely embodying it, we are contemplating the existence of some other mind to observe it and to see in it some revelation of what was in the mind of its maker in fashioning it. And in the mind of the observer a process takes place which also in itself makes everything express something of all existence. For, to 'observe' a thing is more than merely to be aware of it; the difference may be one of degree rather than of kind but when we observe something we are not only conscious of its impact on our minds; the impact evokes a response. We relate it to other contents, to other experiences, of our minds. We co-ordinate it with them. It is thus that we invest it with 'meaning'. When this page lies open before you, for instance, your mind is conscious of the presence of certain black marks on its surface, whether you take notice of them or not. You are then aware of them. When you direct your attention to them, however, you find that they are marks of ink; that they are in certain formations; that they are printed words. You are now not merely aware of them; you are observing them. They express something to you. They express the conception of ink and print. They also express something more. They express thoughts which are in the mind of the writer. When you read a page of music it may express to you a Chopin Polonaise. The music itself may express joy, sorrow, triumph.

And our minds which thus give meaning to a thing by observing it are themselves constituted of the same stuff as the whole universe and are indissolubly one with it. They too hold within themselves potentially something of the whole universe. There are traces and elements in our minds of all existence. So that all our thinking has a universal quality. And thus the meaning with which our minds invest what we observe has a universal quality also. And so it comes that everything doubly expresses for us something of the whole universe. It expresses universality both in itself and in the way our minds deal with it.

The content and the fullness of the expression depend of course both on the observer and on the thing observed. How much the thing succeeds in expressing, how much of univer-

sality is included in it, depends both on the inherent expressive-
ness of the thing and on the experience, the mental development, the education, of the observer. A Latin sonnet, for
instance, expresses nothing of its real meaning to one who
knows no Latin, or an algebraic formula to a man who knows
neither algebra nor arithmetic. We may, for instance, according to our tastes and aptitudes, find more or less of the whole
universe expressing itself in a flower, in a breath-taking view,
in the love of a fellow-being, in the purl of a summer stream,
in azure skies and the tang of the sea, in the spice of adventure,
a snow-crystal, a poem, a picture, or a swelling anthem.

Everything expresses the whole universe, expresses God,
for us in some measure. It expresses some quality or aspect of
the universe with greater or lesser clarity. Only the whole
could fully express the whole. Only God could fully express
God. But there is, for man, nothing in all the world which so
clearly, fully, and successfully expresses so much of the
qualities and aspects of the universe, so much of God, as does
man himself. There is nothing in all creation, for man, so
articulate as man. One living person expresses more than a
whole universe of dead stars and planets moving in their set
courses. As the author of that great Epic of Creation which
ushers in the Book of Genesis puts it, 'God created man in
His own image'. Eternity seeks expression through man,
though it is restricted by the form and limitations of his
physical structure. Indeed one might say that no man has
ever seen so much of God as he has seen in the glimpses of
Him that he has got through what men have said and done
and been—a little from this one, a little from that, a little from
another, and a little perhaps from his own consciousness.

This has important bearings for man. It means that life
is something of a vocation and something of a responsibility
too. God has, as it were, given each of us a commission to
present to the world something of Him—to express some part
or aspect of universal being. We are His stewards and trustees
of all that He has put into the making of us. As we bear ourselves so the world will form some of its conceptions of God,
will gain or lose its ideals, its notions of what life means and
holds, or can hold, for time and eternity.

This is a humbling reflection. Because whatever his race
or colour, his party, creed or character, everyone, even the

very least of men, has such a vocation no less than ourselves. However mean, however low he may have sunk, his capacity to express something of the infinite universe still remains. Its flame may be fanned into life again if it is treated aright by himself and by others. And by creating him with such a capacity, by putting eternity in his heart, God clearly intended that this sacred flame should be so treated.

'Intended' is a legitimate expression to use in this connection. For, since all existence is a unity, since mind and matter are in the final analysis all one stuff, anything we experience in our minds, such as 'intention', can be there only because it is inherent in the very stuff of the universe, in God. And so it is legitimate to express any of the phenomena of nature in terms of their similarity to analogous phenomena of which we are aware in our own minds; and it is equally legitimate to express any of the qualities or aspects of the universe as a whole in such terms. It is legitimate to ascribe to the universe, to God, any or all of the faculties or functions or qualities of mind and personality which we find in ourselves.

Moreover since man is for man the most articulate thing in the world, it is through man that God can most clearly express for men His intentions, His ambitions, for man. Those thoughts and longings that come into our minds, these impulses that arise in our hearts, whence do they come? In the final analysis they can only come from the great universe, from the universal mind. They are God seeking to express Himself through us.

There are no doubt many difficulties and questions which spring to mind about that—questions about the evil that is in man, questions about freedom of will and other things. These will be examined in due course; but meantime it is important to take note that every thought which arises in our mind, if it is of value for men, be it in art, science, philosophy, music, economics, politics, or what not, it is not for our own delectation alone. It is our vocation and duty to impart it to mankind so far as in us lies and circumstances permit.

And even more important is conduct—what we are and what we do, how we bear ourselves before the world. Deeds speak louder than words; and nothing stirs to emulation like kindly behaviour, a heroic deed, a great achievement, a noble character. It behoves us therefore not merely to broadcast our inspirations of mind and heart but to demonstrate our faith in them by acting on them, by trusting our lives to them, by living them. It is only through what men and women express of the infinite universe that mankind can find the way to the 'kingdom of heaven', the realm of bliss, life at its best. And thus too may a man drink deep of the joy of vocation fulfilled.

Thus we see how the diverse views of man are reconciled. A man is an infinitely small part of the infinitely vast universe; but he may express as much of it as the infinite universe, as God, may put into him.

VI. The Meaning of Existence

What is the meaning of existence? Has it any meaning at all? These are problems which have always exercised and perplexed mankind. Some have found an answer to satisfy themselves. Many have despaired of any answer. Much of the difficulty is due to looking at the matter from one or other of two extremes. On the one hand there are people who regard 'meaning' or 'value' as having some absolute quality, as being something which has an independent existence of its own. And then they try to fit the rest of existence into it—to impose it on all existence—and find it hard to do so. On the other hand there are people who think that 'meaning' or 'value' is something which exists only as a conception in our own minds; and they look in vain for any reflection of it in the world outside.

These difficulties are resolved when we recognise that neither 'meaning' nor 'value' nor our own minds nor anything else have in ultimate reality any absolute or independent existence. They are just parts or ingredients of that existence which embraces everything, and every part of which must be constituted of the same kind of stuff, and which must in ultimate reality be a complete and indivisible unity.

However much 'meaning', 'value', 'reason', 'purpose' and such conceptions may appear to be confined to our own minds, we do experience them in our minds; and so to that extent they do exist; and if they exist they must be ingredients in the universal constitution of all that exists. For our minds, like everything else, are just samples of universal existence. They are just parts of that universe which consists of all of which we are aware or could be aware.

On the other hand 'meaning', 'value', and such things are only ingredients like any other. They are just labels which we apply to particular things or particular aspects of things which we experience within our own minds and which must thus be parts or aspects, potentialities or ingredients, of universal existence, neither more nor less than anything else of which we can be aware—heat, for instance, solidity, beauty, electrons, chemical elements, and the whole gamut of existence.

In the light of this it becomes easy to see why it is right to seek a 'meaning' in existence. It is perfectly valid to interpret the universe in terms of any of its constituents—any of its ingredients, or aspects. They are each indissolubly part of the whole; and something of all enters into the make-up of each. All are related to each. We distinguish them as separate entities only by their relations or comparisons with all the others and with the whole; and the differences between things consist in the predominance or development of this element or of that in this thing or in that. And none is in any privileged position. There is none that is absolute, none by which all the others must be judged. Any may with equal validity be used as the subject or reference-frame to which to relate all else. It is perfectly legitimate to describe the whole universe in terms of its relation to any one of them, or, which is the same thing, to describe any one of them in terms of its relation to the whole universe. We are justified for instance in describing the universe in terms of cause and effect, in terms of energy, love, sacrifice, adventure, beauty, value, mind, matter, life, organism, meaning, or any of the myriad other aspects or ingredients which we can find in any of existence. It may not always be easy. It may often be beyond our capacities. But of its validity, so far as we are able to do it, there can be no doubt.

Interpreting the universe then in terms of 'meaning', what is the meaning, what is the purpose, of existence? It is a question to which no man could hope to give even a remotely complete answer. One might as well ask a nerve-cell in a man's brain, if it could speak, to explain the man and what he does, to describe all that goes on in his mind, all his hopes and ambitions, his likes and dislikes, the mainsprings of his life. Only it would be infinitely more impossible for a mere man to comprehend all that is in the mind of the vast, infinite, universe. His mind is such an infinitesimal scrap of the universe and only the whole could fully understand the whole.

But there are some things about the matter which do

present themselves even to our limited understandings. One of these is that there can be nothing ulterior about the purposes of the universe, about God's purposes. They cannot have anything to do with any other existence, with anything or any being outside the universe, outside God; because there is none. So whatever universal existence—whatever God— does must be of His own volition and for His own purposes alone. He must do it because He wants to do it. Otherwise He simply would not do it. It must be entirely for His own good pleasure. Whatever He does must be done for its own sake, for the joy of doing it. It must be an end in itself.*

That is not to say of course that God eschews all pain and unpleasantness. Like a musician practising his instrument, or a golfer practising his strokes, He may quite deliberately undertake something which is unpleasant or even painful for a time, for the sake of the joy it will ultimately bring to Him. The joy of God need not be haphazard. It may be planned. Indeed since it is so in that little bit of the universe of which we have direct knowledge, our own selves, it would appear that such planning is normal throughout the universe. But it can only be for the sake of some over-all satisfaction, some ultimate joy, to be achieved by it. The whole universe is enjoying itself. That is one thing which existence means. So even though we may suffer tortures untold, though empires may fall and civilisations perish, and though worlds may crash and suns explode, we can rest assured that it works out in God's hands for the ultimate good and joy of all.

Another thing which even to our limited minds seems clear is that existence cannot be static; the universe can have no pleasure in anything which is fixed and unchanging. This too we can deduce from our own experience, limited as it is. Deep down in our hearts is something which demands change, life. Anything which is unchanging becomes monotonous and finally ceases to interest or even to attract attention. It loses all ability to create pleasure. It becomes dead. Since this

* Is it necessary to remind the reader that this, and what follows in this chapter, is a metaphorical mode of expression, adopted for the sake of brevity and cogency, and that the propositions which it lays down are intended only as approximations to the truth, because we do not know how far our modes of thought are applicable beyond the world of observation and experience?

is an essential element of our own consciousness it must reflect something which holds throughout the universe. There can be no pleasure in what is static and dead. God must be a living God. There can be no finality or perfection—not even for God. For the achievement of a perfection that was perpetual would mean unending monotony. It would be an end of living. It would be death. God must be creating, developing, improving, exploring, experimenting, inventing, searching out new pleasures and thrills, much as men invent games, for the sheer joy of it, savouring them to the uttermost, and discarding what has become dead or using it as a stepping stone to new creations.

And so although existence must hold treasures of meaning far beyond our comprehension, here at least is something which must be part of its meaning. God must be seeking joy in living, joy without stint or measure. He must be revelling in the sheer joy of life.

This little bit of the universe which we know and live in, this world of ours, must be a great adventure of God's. He must have created it and all that is in it, and go on creating and maintaining it, for the sheer joy of it. Among all the other things which it contains He must have created man with all his faculties and powers for the joy that He can have through the lives and joys, the experiences, the personalities, of men and women. It is through us, in our joy, that God is seeking joy in this little corner of creation. However good a man may be, however wide his talents and opportunites, or however humble and restricted his life, every thought, every creation of his heart, every joy and every sorrow, touch an answering chord in the heart of the universe, in the heart of God. It must be in order that He may savour the joy of such things that God has made man.

And that equally applies to the whole of creation, to all nature. It may be that there is a different quality, or a different intensity, in the joy afforded by one being than by another; but God must feel all the pain and all the joy that all living things feel. How then does it come that there is pain and evil, sorrow and ugliness, in the world? That is indeed a pertinent and insistent question, and it will be dealt with in due course.

VII. The Purpose of Life

It is sometimes said that the purpose of life is to afford an educational process for the formation of character. But character is not an end in itself. It is only a means to an end. Its object is the fitting of our spiritual resources to deal appropriately with the life and environment in which we are placed. And so the purpose of the character to be acquired in this life is said to be to fit us for life beyond the grave.

No doubt in God's plans this world may serve some such ulterior aim; but for us humans such ideas must be pure speculation. We know that the origins of each one of us, as integral parts of the universe, must go right back into the infinity and eternity before we were born; that the roots of our being here and now must stretch right out into infinity and eternity; that in our make-up there must be traces of all the qualities inherent in the infinite and eternal universe of which we are parts; and that into infinity and eternity we must return when this life is over. From God we came and to God we shall return. But for the moment, here and now in this present life, we are shut off from the knowledge of what conditions were or are or shall be in that infinity and eternity which lies behind and beyond our present life. And on what these conditions are depends the kind of character which will suit them. Of what use, for instance, is a gentle and reflective character to a soldier on the battlefield? Of what use a sensitive love of beauty in the hurly burly of the business world? How unfitted for the ordinary life of this world does a nun become after years of cloistered seclusion! What kind of character will be needed in the life beyond?

It seems clear that for us humans at any rate God sets no such impossible task. He appears rather to have been at pains to shut us off from all possibility of being distracted in the pursuit of our lives in this present world by any knowledge of what went before and what comes after or what lies beyond.

It is not of course impossible, if not very probable, that

proper scientific psychic research may some day succeed in penetrating that veil to some extent; but the results so far achieved in this way are too scanty and too trivial to have any serious influence on one's plan of life. That being so, it seems clear that we humans must seek all the purposes of this life, not in preparation for some achievement in some other life, but within the bounds of this present life and this physical universe in which we find ourselves.

No sooner has this been said than it seems plain that the only purpose can be to achieve the greatest possible joy—and to achieve it here and now in this present life—for ourselves and for all who are involved in it. Since, as we have seen, we are integral parts of all existence and there is in each of us something of all that there is in all existence, and since the meaning of all existence is the joy of living, that too must be the dominant purpose of the life that is ours. And indeed we are all aware that deeply planted in our hearts is the over powering urge to live, to create joy. And this confirms what reason would lead us to conclude, that it must be God's intention that we should do so. We have as it were to carry on within the limits of life in this little corner of the universe the process of life, the process of creation, which God is pursuing in infinity and eternity in the great universe. It is as though God had handed over to us to carry on His activities within the limits of this world, had committed to us to make the best we can of the materials He has created and put at our disposal —the physical world, including ourselves, our human bodies and personalities with all their instincts and needs and potentialities. It is God's purpose that with these materials we should create all the joys that are possible so that He may enjoy them through us.

The joy we are to seek is thus not for ourselves alone but for all who are involved in the life of this world. That includes not only every man, woman, and child, but every sentient creature, according to the measure of its capacity to feel; because they, one and all, are expressions of God, who made them, in and through which God feels too. This includes the whole animal kingdom; and who knows where we can draw the line?

The purpose of life for us therefore would appear to be to devote ourselves to such things as, here and now in this present life, are worth while for their own sakes—things which for each of us are ends in themselves. The scope and variety of such things are limited only by the capacity of the human heart for feeling and of the human mind for understanding. They may not be the same for one man as for another; but they include such things as the simple joys of home, love, and family, social intercourse, the sense of physical well-being, the enjoyment of nature, travel and discovery, music, painting, poetry, drama, religion, scientific research, invention, sports, games and pastimes, all the things which make life worth while, the alleviation of suffering, and hosts of other things, both those we already have and those yet to be discovered or invented—anything which increases the sum of human happiness, anything which for human beings is an end in itself. In other words the purpose of life is to retain as far as possible throughout life the child-like spirit, the spirit which tries things out, which probes and investigates, which does things with fascinated absorption without any ulterior purpose but simply because they are worth while in themselves. And the highest peaks of human joy are found when we commit ourselves with single-minded abandon to some end which holds our passionate devotion, some end to attain which we would spend and sacrifice, some end for which we would cast all else to the winds and imperil life itself. It is then that we most truly live. It is then we must fully express God. 'No man having put his hand to the plough, and looking back, is fit for the kingdom of God.'

That does not mean of course that the true purpose of life involves the shunning of all suffering and unpleasantness. Indeed the joys of life at their best can be won only through planning and striving and effort, through suffering and unpleasantness; and the most worth-while things have only been attained for mankind through heroic pioneer sacrifice. But it does mean that we are to pursue life here and now in this present life without thought of any gain in a future life either in character or in circumstances or any other way, and be content to know that the ordering of life beyond is in the hands of God.

The means to an end, however, often hold some quality of an end in itself. There is a joy for instance in just learning to do anything, in the acquisition of knowledge or skill, in new experiences, in efficiency. Religion, for instance, which, however important, is primarily only a means to an end—the refreshing and restoring of the spirit to fit it for the business of life—is also in some measure an end in itself, to be enjoyed for its own sake like music, drama, literature or art. But however much we plan and sacrifice, our ultimate aims are intended to be things which are ends in themselves, ends in this present life.

Nor of course does this mean that we are each to seek our own joy above all else. It must indeed be a basic duty of each one of us to tend and enjoy that marvellous instrument for living which has been entrusted to our care and keeping in the shape of our own physical and spiritual beings, and to develop it to the full. It is to each of us that has been committed the primary responsibility for the welfare of his own body and personality. Without that instrument we could achieve nothing in this world. But it is the common experience of mankind that, paradoxically, we achieve the fullest joy when we most forget ourselves in seeking the joy of others—in seeking our own joy through enjoying the joy of others—by the way of love. So that to whatever we devote our efforts we can only achieve the fullest joy through it when we seek to savour its joy through others' enjoyment of it. It is not merely because we thus enlarge the sphere of our joying. It goes deeper than that. It is just what we would expect from the structure of existence; for it is then that we most fully express the something of universal existence which is in us all. It is then that we come nearest to the way in which God enjoys life, however vast the difference between our little effort and God's. For God not only enjoys the things He has created, and enjoys the creating of them; He also gets joy through the joys of the sentient beings and living spirits which He has created. Only the whole—only God—can have the most complete joy in living. But the nearer we approach, however little it be, to the way God lives the more joy we can have.

Nor does it mean that we can enjoy these ends without subordinating our own ends to the common weal, without co-operating with our fellow beings or without training our spirits, fashioning our characters, to be fit instruments for such a purpose. But the ultimate purpose of this life, from which nothing should be suffered to deflect us, must be to do the best that in us lies to contribute towards making the best of this world for all that participate in it.

Man can never reach finality however; he can never reach enduring perfection in his affairs any more than can God Himself. In the very achievement of the ideal he has sought there are the germs of decay, of growing imperfection through familiarity and monotony. The urge in him to create, which is life, impels him to seek ever new achievements. He must go on seeking, improving, creating—seeking life abundant and ever renewed—or assuredly he will cease to live. The emergence and development of reason in man opened up a vast field for such life—a field the limits of which are not in sight; but it is only one of many. There are also, for instance, imagination (art in all its forms), faith, love—fields for limitless adventures of the spirit.

As the Westminster Divines so succinctly put it in the *Shorter Catechism*, 'Man's chief end is to glorify God and to enjoy Him for ever'. When we keep in view all the universal meaning which the term God holds, this can only mean that man's chief end is to make that part of the universe, physical and spiritual, in which God has placed him more glorious by constantly creating new joys out of it in every possible way. There is no other way in which we can 'glorify' God—in fact and deed as distinct from mere words. Unfortunately that great truth has too often been whittled away, and what remains side-tracked, by seeking to confine it to religious activities. Important as these are, they are only part of the life to which God has called us, and not even the most important part, being in themselves only a means to other ends.

Nor can we ever get away from the fact that we are parts of the infinite and eternal, that we have our lot and part in the universe, that this life is not all, that it is only a point in infinity, an incident in eternity. Nor is this world some alien affair in which we have somehow become involved without our consent. We have a proprietary interest in the physical world and all that it contains and in the success of God's great adventure of Man. And so—call it conscience or call it what you will—a sense of all this consciously or subconsciously ever permeates our beings, whether we understand its origins or not; and it can never be wholly ignored. At times it is apt to flare into a consuming fire and dominate all our being; and always it gives a quality to all our strivings and all our life. If we yield to it, it means that there are some things we cannot do, and some things that life cannot do to us. It tends to give us poise and calm; and we cannot worthily face the testing moments of life or rise to heights of true greatness unless we are consciously attuned to it. The situation is like that of a man playing a game. If he would make the best of it he must go all out to win; but he must abide by the rules of the game and he must seek no ends ulterior to those of the game itself. And he may be completely absorbed in the game, and yet all the while his conduct is restrained by the knowledge that this game is just an incident in his life, and that there is all his life which has gone before it and all his life to live after it, and that even now there is his life all around outside the game, including perhaps interested spectators. And so he is impelled, cost what it may, to play fair; and he takes all the fortunes of the game with a good grace.

So whatever remote purposes God may have in His own heart, beyond human ken, life for us is meant to be a glorious adventure, fit for the sons and daughters of the Infinite and Eternal, the Ever-creating—fit for the children of the living God.

In short, the purpose of life is to live.

VIII. Moral Law

Co-operation is essential to all progress in human affairs. Mankind may have been slow to recognise this, but the history of human progress from the jungle onwards throughout the ages is largely the story of how men did come to recognise the value of co-operating with each other first in one sphere and then in another. It is thus that civilisation has evolved.

It is not merely a case of recognising that greater efficiency, better output, can be attained by team-work, by co-operation. Men feel that there is something more involved than mere efficiency. We have a feeling that we are 'entitled' to a measure of co-operation, and entitled to it both from the universe in which we live and from other men, even if it amounts to no more than just to abstain from interfering with us and our activities and possessions. And this inevitably involves the corollary that we have a feeling that we on our part 'owe' the like to them. In other words, we are conscious of a moral sense. And the fact that we do experience that sense in our hearts and minds shows that it must be something which is inherent in the very stuff of the universe. It could not otherwise emerge within these little samples of all existence which our minds are.

The existence of this moral sense in our consciousness should be no mystery or enigma. It is just what one would expect when one bears in mind that in the final analysis we are all of one common stuff—mind, matter, man, nature, the vast universe, past, present and future, in one great, infinite, eternal, ever-living and ever-creating unity; that we are all partners in a common adventure. It would be strange indeed if some consciousness of this did not break through the barriers of our individuality and isolation. Consciously or subconsciously we are aware that, whatever the barriers of space and time and matter between us, other men and the spiritual and natural world around us are, like ourselves, part of that vast unity— indissolubly part of it and part of ourselves; that their lot and destiny is cast in the same infinite and eternal unity as ours and is therefore a matter of concern to us, just as our lot and destiny is a matter of concern to that great unity and to them.

Moreover since it is only by co-operating with other men and with the natural and spiritual resources at our disposal that we can satisfy the urge within us to live, to create, and to savour the joy of doing it, it is just as one would expect that we should feel that it is a matter of concern to them (other men and our natural and spiritual environment) to co-operate with us to that end, and that we should feel 'entitled' to their co-operation and under 'obligation' to render a like service to them, in seeking joy for all who participate in the life and fortune of this world.

This feeling, this moral sense, it should be observed in passing, is not confined to human relations. It equally applies to the physical world of our environment, and to the spiritual world in which we feel we have our being. We have a feeling, for instance, that the physical world which has given us birth owes us something; and we have a feeling that the spiritual world in which we have our roots should be willing to help us. And so it is a natural instinct to pray.

Without such a moral sense, without such a sense of obligation, the full benefits of co-operation cannot be attained. Man, it is true, can be driven or enticed into co-operating with other men by compulsion or by hope of gain of one sort of another, physical, economic, or otherwise; but without some measure of willingness in the co-operation its outcome is unsatisfactory and sooner or later the co-operation itself breaks down. The fullest results can only be attained by willing co-operation, fortified it may be by love. A contract, for instance, which is not backed by a sense of moral obligation is an unreliable affair. And even in co-operating with nature some such similar feeling for nature is necessary if man is to achieve the fullest co-operation with the natural world around him. Doctors, scientists, research workers, agriculturists, tenders of animals—all are aware of this; and everyone has some experience of it even if it be only in the tending of his own physical body. And in the spiritual sphere too, whether in our relations with other people or with the greater spiritual world, in prayer for instance or in religion, the same sense of willing co-operation or love, is essential for success.

Thus there have gradually evolved the moral codes of the world. At different times, in different ages and places, mankind has been pursuing different projects which for the time being they had come to accept as contributing to the sum-total of man's enjoyment of life; and they have recognised that co-operation was necessary to achieve these projects. And so has been born the sense that all the people concerned 'owed' it to each other and to the community concerned to contribute their part to this end. A moral law has come into being.

There must however be as many different conceptions of which projects are worth while as there are different personalities in the world. So there has to be co-operation not only in the pursuit of the project in hand but in selecting the project to be pursued. There must be some pooling of ideas and ideals—the sacrificing of something here and something there of individual aims, a certain concentration on this and that, from time to time, out of the common pool—if chaos is to be avoided and something worth while achieved. There are many ways in which mankind has from time to time selected the projects on which to concentrate. Perhaps a man of genius has had an inspiration of outstanding merit for his place and time which has won its way to general acceptance. Or a great statesman has succeeded in imposing some advance in human well-being on his people. Or perhaps a community have consciously elected to pursue a particular end, or to pursue it in a particular way, as is done in a democracy. Thus for instance the advantage of security of person and property has come to be recognised, the advantage of the family, the tribe, the nation* as units of society; the advantages of agriculture, of specialisation in arts and crafts, of trade, of measures for the control of disease, have come to be recognised and accepted

* This view involves that too much importance has sometimes been attached to the State in one meaning or another, as the focus of moral obligation, by philosophers, from Hobbes onwards. On close scrutiny of the moral sense, the State would appear to be only one of many groups or institutions claiming moral allegiance; and often it is not even the most important. The Roman Catholic church, for instance, is larger and more wide-spread than any single State, and its claims to moral allegiance have sometimes been put before those even of nationality by its adherents. Wherever people come together in some common project the moral sense comes into play—a group spirit—even if it be only a fortuitous collection of people on a bus tour.

as aims to be pursued in common; and the co-operation necessary to secure them has been accepted also, and so has become part of the moral code of a community.

The full riches of life can be attained moreover only when everybody contributes all he can to the common stock. Everyone's potentialities must be evoked and developed. No doubt a man's soul is inviolable; only he himself can develop the potentialities that have been vouchsafed to him; that is why there are limits to what can be achieved by merely compulsory co-operation. But others can help him. They can help to ensure that his environment is one in which development is possible. They can give him incentives to develop. They can help by education, by encouragement, and by example. And so such things are among those to which mankind's co-operation must extend.

Sometimes the rules of the moral code have depended for their binding force only on the realisation of their practical convenience; sometimes on the inner feelings, the conscience, of men, the sense of the need for co-operation; sometimes religion has adopted them and has reinforced them by its own sanctions; and sometimes the State has taken them up and has made them the law of the land. But to whatever they owe their compulsion it is always the human need which gives them their shape and their reality.

And so the process has gone on, extending and becoming more complex with the growth of civilisation until now, like the structure of our civilisation, the moral code is highly complex. Some of its rules have less importance than others; and some have won more general acceptance than others. But there are some which, because they stem from the laws of nature and their associated instincts, or through long and general experience, or in one way or another, have come to be recognised as fundamental to our existing civilisation, the basis on which it is built and without which it would collapse. These form the core of the current moral code, such as the Ten Commandments.

As sex morality has come so much under public scrutiny recently, it may be worth examining what has just been said with special regard to chastity. The rule of chastity is no invention of man. It is fundamentally derived from the fact that man is a monogamous animal, and so nature has endowed him with all the powerful instincts required to secure that pattern of life. Nature, of course, is not concerned with any rites of marriage: the sex act itself creates the union. It is true that man can and does break away from his natural instincts in the process of creating, or evolving, his own way of life, his own civilisation. But there are limits to the extent that this can be done at any one stage in his self-evolution without creating havoc and causing untold suffering. And while we have already modified nature's institution of monogamy (for instance, by introducing marriage and divorce laws) to suit our present stage of civilisation, the original instincts are still so powerful that their disregard almost invariably inflicts infinite pain on some of the people concerned. Moreover the instincts are reinforced by the physiological facts of life. The family also is the basis of our civilisation, and the family is very dependent on the monogamistic way of life. These are the things which are the bases of our code of sex morality.

Such co-operation is thus one of the prime necessities of human life. The moral sense is no creation of man's imagination. It is a manifestation of that unity of all existence from which we can never wholly escape. And without yielding to it nothing effective can be achieved in human affairs. But the channels into which it is directed, the forms in which it expresses itself—these are spheres in which man has wide scope for his creative faculty. They are very largely matters of his own devising.

In this respect the moral sense is at one with our other emotions and fundamental instincts. The desire for joy, for instance, is no creation of man's fancy; but the forms in which he can give expression to it are things of his own choosing and largely of his own creating. The gregarious instinct is born with him; but he chooses for himself the ways in which he gives it play, and they are of his own creating—social gatherings, clubs, sports, and all the rest. The love of beauty is inherent in man; but the ways in which he gives it play are of his own choosing, and the ways in which he expresses it are of his own creating. The urge to live is fundamental to man's being; but the shaping of his life is in his own hands.

And so it is with the moral sense. It is something which is born with him and is inherent in his being; but it is man himself who chiefly shapes the channels in which it flows, who creates the forms in which it is expressed, who turns it to further the ends of life. The need for co-operation is fundamental to the life of man; but it is man who decides in what ways and to what ends co-operation with his fellow-men shall be applied; and that is what determines the forms of the resultant moral codes.

The moral sense is thus, on this view, not a matter of the reason. It cannot be resolved by moral judgments alone. It is fundamentally an instinct or emotion. But the channels into which it is directed, the ways in which and the ends for which it is used, are matters to be determined by reason.

It is inevitable that we should seek some short and simple phrase in which to express such complex ideas in ordinary conversation; and it is singularly apt to describe the moral sense as being an expression of the will of God. Like love, for instance, it is peculiarly associated with the unifying principle of all existence as distinct from the separate aims of individuals. But this does not alter the fundamental fact of man's free-will. It is to man that God has committed the working out of life in this human world; and it is man, in so working it out, who has created these moral codes, and created them for his—for man's—own purposes. They are the rules of conduct to which it is necessary, as a practical matter, for humans to conform in order to achieve the co-operation required for the projects which man is, by common consent, for the benefit of mankind, pursuing at the moment.

It is the function of man to take life in both hands and shape it to his own conceptions, in one direction here, in another there, and to keep on shaping and reshaping it and refashioning it, so as to keep on getting abundant interest and enjoyment in the doing of it. Nor can there be in mankind's collective affairs, any more than in those of individual men or in those of God, any finality, any perfection. In the very achievement of its aims they begin to pall. There must be ever change, creation, life.

Therefore while the moral sense itself—the sense of obligation, of owing and being entitled to something—is a thing which is fundamental and eternally implanted in the heart of man, the moral codes which spring from it are different. There are not many of their rules which are forever fixed and unchangeable laws for man. Some, like honesty, loyalty, chastity, respect for life, are fundamental to any worthwhile relations between human beings, any worth-while co-operation. But as regards the others, since man has devised them for his own use so man may and must revise and discard and add to them as his ever-changing circumstances and needs require. 'The sabbath was made for man, and not man for the sabbath. Therefore man* is lord also of the sabbath.'

That is not to say that any man or group of men, or even mankind as a whole, can play fast and loose with existing moral codes without doing violence to the moral sense. It is part and parcel of every moral code that its rules are not to be tampered with or put aside until the human need which brought them into being has ceased to exist, or until something equally good or better has been found to put in their place. For it is on these moral codes that our whole civilisation is built, and it would collapse if they were weakened or destroyed. They do not depend for their authority on any superstition or on any religion. They are the fundamentals on which our existing form of civilisation depends. That is their authority, practical and moral. Any self-repression or self-sacrifice which their observance entails is the price which we pay for the benefits of civilisation. Any attempt to evade paying that price, without good and sufficient cause, while enjoying these benefits, is a fraud on society. It also wreaks violence on our moral sense, on our inner being, our partnership in the universe, our kinship with God.

Nor must it be forgotten that it is not only to other men that man has moral obligations. For the same reasons, though in differing degree, they bind him to everything in the world, in the physical and spiritual world in which we find ourselves; for these things are all expressions of the same God who has expressed Himself through man. Man has moral obligations to his own physical body, to his mind and personality, with all their complex of instincts and inherited traits, to nature and the physical world, and to all living, sentient, creatures. They all claim to be brought within the scope of his care and planning. The man who has no feeling for the beauty of nature, no

* The expression 'the son of man', used for that last 'man' in the Authorised Version of the Bible (Mark II, 27, 28) is just the idiom for 'man' in the Aramaic language in which Jesus spoke.

love for animals, in whom no answering chord responds to their joys and their pains, is no true son of God.

Such being the structure of moral law, conflicts of loyalty and duty are bound to arise. Thence come some of the greatest trials and tragedies of the human race. There are conflicts for instance as between loyalty to the ties of family and duty to the wider community; between duty to this group and to that; or between fidelity to one's vision of the long-term good of the whole family of mankind on the one hand, and duty to the more immediate interests of one's group or community, one's nation or race, on the other. Instances could be multiplied indefinitely; but it is such problems as these which create the biggest temptations which arise in the heart of man. The Temptation of our Lord, when the 'devil' showed Him 'all the kingdoms of the world', was of such a kind. It is presented as no crude choice between self-aggrandisement and selfless service of mankind. That would have presented no temptation to one of His character.

And besides all these conflicts which arise within the heart of the individual man there are conflicts of interest and aim which lead to clashes between this group and that, between this movement and that. There are conflicts for instance between church and state, between political parties, between ideologies, between nations, and between races. Such conflicts have been the curse of humanity, wreaking untold havoc and frustration on the human race, and threatening constantly to obliterate all human achievement. And it must ever remain so, with mankind blundering from one tragedy to another as it gropes towards the light, till it has devised some means of harmonising all these conflicting aims and interests.

It is not only for the urgent and obvious negative purpose of preventing the misery, the destruction and slaughter, aroused by war and strife that such a code of world morality is needed. It is no less necessary for the positive purpose of providing the best opportunity for everybody for the harmonious development of all those things on which worthwhile human life and achievement depend. For this purpose co-operation between groups and nations and races is clearly no less necessary than it is between individual men. And so mankind can never rest until it has evolved a satisfactory master plan—some kind of super-state perhaps—accepted by all the world, within the framework of which all lesser plans and ploys, groups and institutions, loyalties and duties, nations, races, and states will find their appropriate place in harmonious co-operation for the common weal.

The turbulence of the world in this present age is largely due to gropings after such a master plan; and its troubles may well be the birth-pangs of a new and better age.

IX. Sin, Suffering and Free-will

From time immemorial people have been perplexed by the problem of the existence of suffering and wrong in the world. How can there be a God when such things exist? How can there be a power that is both omnipotent and good, by whom the world was designed and by whom it is controlled? Is not the existence of suffering and wrong fundamentally inconsistent with the rule of reason and right, with any kind of order?

One might answer these problems in the way the drama of Job does, by saying that they are beyond the mind of man to understand; that the answer depends on ultimate realities which lie beyond the scope of the human mind; that the defects we see are not in God's universe but only in our conceptions of it. The defects, the seeming inconsistencies, are only in the patterns or models of ultimate realities which we have created for ourselves. We cannot know enough about the ultimate realities themselves to be able to detect any faults in them. We can only accept God's universe on faith.

Another way however to answer is to revise our models. It is to show, if we can, that there is a plan which *might* be true in ultimate reality (which God *may* have adopted for His universe) and which if true would offer a reasonable explanation of these seeming contradictions. And that is the method we will follow here.

The conception of the wholeness of the universe, which has been followed out in the preceding pages, is one such plan, and it has its own solution to offer for such problems. It is perhaps hardly necessary to remind the reader that this conception is not something which is claimed to have been established, something completely valid in ultimate reality. Such things *are* beyond the scope of the human mind. Only Universal Mind could know them because only Universal Mind is comprehensive enough to embrace them and so to experience them. The conception is in reality no more than a mode of thought, a model or reference-frame, to help us to focus our thoughts on such matters; but it is one which, as we have seen, appears to fit such facts as are ascertainable with sufficient accuracy to be useful as a model. If such a conception can provide a solution to these problems about suffering and wrong and free-will, that is all that is required, because the problems do not call for a demonstration (which would be impossible) of how these things are in fact reconciled in our world, but only of how such a reconciliation is reasonably possible. It may be noted however that if the conception does afford a solution of these problems that would enhance its value as a useful model.

A complete unity, with nothing else to compare it with, a unity of all existence, could only be observed by features in it. If it contained no features it would just be a blank, sheer nothingness. On the other hand, since it is a unity features could not constitute any absolute divisions in it. That would be inconsistent with its unity. So features in it could only consist of relative differences, differences between this part and that—more of this quality, for instance, in this part and of that quality in another part, or relative differences of location in space and time (or what corresponds to such things in ultimate reality), something like waves on the surface of the ocean. In other words, everything existing within it (that is, everything in the whole universe) would be relative, have only a relative existence, would consist of relativities, with no real absolutes anywhere except the fact of existence itself. 'I am that I am.' And this applies to happenings and action, to emotions, to everything which can be experienced in the human mind, no less than to static features. They would none of them be absolute, clear-cut, entities. They would all have their counter-parts (from which they differ) either in some other entity (like one wave compared with another) or in all the rest of the universe, from which they can be distinguished. And they would also have much in common with their counterparts; the differences would not be absolute.

Any action, for instance, always has its counterpart which resists change. Action assumes effort; action without effort of some sort is meaningless; it would be inaction, passive submission to conditions as they are. And effort implies something to be overcome, resistance. In mechanics it is called inertia. And something similar would be involved in everything that happens in all existence. It is the element of unity which would pervade everything, hold everything together, despite differences. The moral sense would be an instance of it.

Sin is a failure of the moral sense. The moral sense would not be something absolute, something self-existing, in this view. Even if it is something in the sphere of the emotions rather than of reason or the will, it would be the element of unity in that sphere, the element which resists differentiation and disruption, which resists any excess of individualisation. If there is to be in existence a being (man) with a measure of creative urge which can have scope for expression, a being with any freedom of will so that he seeks to express himself, to develop his own individuality, then there must also be scope for the operation of this restraining influence to prevent him carrying his individualisation, his separating activity, too far. But it could not be an absolute restriction, or there could be no freedom of will for him. Like everything else in all existence, it would have to be relative. A balance must be found between unity and diversity which best serves man's ends; and, if there is to be freedom of will, it must be left to each individual to decide how far he will yield to the urge for unity and how far he will yield to the urge for his own unrestricted self-seeking. If he yields too far to the individualising urge it becomes moral failure or sin. But it would be all in keeping with the kind of order that prevails throughout all existence. The existence of sin and moral failure would be no enigma. It would be no more mysterious or incompatible with the rule of law than the fact that inertia (in physical mechanics) does not prevent a destructive explosion. The universe would be ordered so.

The problem of suffering and pain is in an analogous position. As we have seen, everything we do involves effort of some kind. Effort to overcome some resistance. And an effort implies some discomfort at least, something in itself unwanted, which the will has to force one to accept for the sake of achieving something which one does want. And discomfort is just a name for comparatively slight pain. It is only a matter of degree. Pain must consequently be an integral element in every act throughout the universe, in all creation, in all life. Its presence is in keeping with the kind of order which, in this view, would rule throughout all existence.

In the infinite complications of life the operation of this element of pain would become infinitely complex. If we find it sometimes difficult to recognise its manifestations we need only reflect that the physical world in all its infinite variety and abundance is a product of various arrangements and combinations of that minute, tenuous, whirling, body, the atom, and reflect also how difficult it is to realise that fact. And if sometimes pain obtrudes itself in forms for which we find it hard to believe that there can be any meaning or purpose, we need only reflect what takes place in our own bodies. Our every act and movement, however pleasant to us, involves suffering to thousands of living cells which compose our bodies and which are parts of ourselves—to some of them, death. *You* have no doubt about the pleasantness or rightness of your action, but could the cell, if it had a reasoning mind, fathom the purpose of its suffering or the need for it?

The conception of the unity of all existence, paradoxically, helps also in the understanding of how freedom is possible in an ordered universe. The conceptions of will, and of freedom of will, are complex, but they predominantly involve the conception of control. Without attempting to analyse them further, they have no meaning except by reference to something which resists them, something which they have to overcome. When will comes into operation within a complete unity, existence has as it were to be divided into two parts, the one active and the other negative, which are not completely separate but only relatively different—the will and the element of resistance, the element which seeks to maintain unity. The will is not absolute, so it may be relatively more predominant here than there. There are always elements of similarity, the elements which maintain the unity, as well as difference, in both will and resistance. And in the same way the element of will, of control, may itself be divided into different parts, with reference to particular bases of differentiation (for example, laws of nature, cosmic mechanics, vegetation, animal life, human life) each relatively confined to some particular sphere of existence but maintaining their continuity, their element of unity. And so the unity of the whole, the ordering of the control of the whole, is not lost. The operation of will in individual men might be on some such basis. The individual would have a limited autonomy within himself, a controlling power in reference to particular aspects of his constitution, relatively free from the controlling power of universal will, but only relatively, while the universal element of resistance would operate in him too, maintaining the continuity of control with universal control or will. Cross waves on the sea represent something like the pattern contemplated. And so man's freedom of will within limits would not be inconsistent with an ordered pattern of control throughout the universe.

We cannot leave this subject however without noticing a difficulty of another kind which is sometimes felt about the existence of free-will. It is associated, not with the conception of the will of God, of an ordered universe, but with the nature of time, with the sequence of events. There are phenomena which might seem to support the proposition that the whole course of our lives is mapped out beforehand, is predetermined or, as theologians say, fore-ordained. There are, for instance, such things as the kind of dream described by J. W. Dunne in *An Experiment with Time*, in which future events are witnessed; and there are people who, whether in dream or not, can apparently see future happenings. We call them prophets. If our lives are thus ordered in advance how can that be reconciled with freedom of will on our part, or with moral responsibility?

The existentialist conception of complete freedom for man appears to be self-contradictory. To find all that is contained in any existence it has to be compared not only with other existences but with non-existence, which is the alternative to existence. Now non-existence may have perfect freedom in the sense of being free from all restrictions (except that implied in the fact of existence) but non-existence can have no feelings, no knowledge, no reason, no ability to make choices, no ability to utilise a world of existence around it. Each and all of such mechanisms or processes would limit its perfect nothingness and hence its freedom. And yet these are just the things which existentialism assumes for man before he begins to exist, to make choices. Existentialist man is placed in the world with his freedom already restricted by these functions; in other words he is a man and not, say, an ape. His 'essence' is at any rate partly defined before he can make any choice. The difference between man and other things in this respect is not absolute as existentialism propounds. It appears rather to be only relative. We have (or seem to have) more of the creative urge, the ability to choose, and less of the 'essence' or limiting definition, than for instance other animals or a tree; but the limitation is there. Existentialism seems to recognise something of this limitation in the conception that when I choose, I choose for all men. This involves that the choices of all men in some measure limit my freedom of choice.

The solution seems to lie in the conception of the wholeness of the universe. Under that conception traces of all these things (freedom, restriction, etc.) are included in everything, some predominating more than others. Life consists in harmonising them. In final analysis this consists, as Hegel said, in synthesising thesis and antithesis—much as a zip fastener works, tying up the paradoxes which lie at the core of all existence.

Moreover existentialists assume that the aim of all man's striving is to attain freedom. Why? To what end? The only aim about which such questions are meaningless, the only aim which is an end in itself, is gladness of heart. So that must be the aim of all human endeavour. And man has all these things at his disposal to use to attain that end, within the limitations of his situation.

If, as we have seen, time is no self-existent, no absolute thing but a created, relative thing like everything else in the physical world; if past, present, and future are not absolute but relative matters depending on the will of Universal Being; and if our individuality is also relative; if we are each in ultimate reality parts of the whole; if we each have our lot and part in Universal Being; then the difficulty of understanding the matter may not disappear but the irreconcilability does. It is, in this view, our conceptions of time and of individuality that are inadequate and need to be revised. However difficult it may be for us to grasp the conception, we ourselves have our lot and part in shaping our destiny whether from past, present, or future, whether predetermined or not.*

But however inadequate our theories and conceptions may be, and however incomplete our knowledge, over-riding all other considerations there remains the fact that we do experience what seems to us to be freedom of will, and that this is the only complete and direct knowledge we have of any will, and the only source from which we derive the very conception either of will or of freedom of will. While it is, as we have seen, possible that what it seems to us to be is a reality, we have no means of knowing whether the experience is true or whether it only seems to us to be true while in reality all our willing is determined for us. In these circumstances the only reasonable thing for us to do is to behave as though it were completely true in ultimate reality and yield to the urge of our innermost beings to use the means at our disposal to express ourselves and so find joy.

* Kant's conception of time, as being as it were part of our mental equipment, would seem to lead to a somewhat similar solution. Time would lose its importance in the shaping of events. It would only affect the way they *appear* to us. What is the reality behind the appearance would remain unknown to us.

X. Prayer

One of the devices now in the hands of psychiatrists makes use of electricity in the diagnosis of mental states. It records electro-magnetic radiations from the brain, and their variations according to the various activities of the brain. In face of scientific knowledge and experience in this and many other spheres, it seems odd that there should any longer be any scepticism about the possibility, at any rate, of telepathy and prayer (which are but two instances of the same thing). We know enough about the transmission and reception of electro-magnetic waves, in connection with radio and television, to realise how much more there is to know about such matters. In the light of such things it is easier to realise how very possible it may be that one human mind can communicate with another, properly attuned to it, or could broadcast its thoughts and desires so that they would reach some other mind. The influence of the cerebral radiations on the electro-magnetic field surrounding the brain is slight; but it shows that the state of the mind does in fact affect the field.

It thus seems clear that scientifically it is not merely possible but entirely probable that human minds can communicate in such ways with each other, and that the human mind can communicate with the world around it, and conversely that the universe can communicate with the human mind. It may well be that some birds and animals thus communicate with the flock or herd, and that man has largely lost a faculty for doing so through disuse.

In the scheme of things deduced philosophically, to which we have been referring in previous chapters, it is not only not surprising that minds could thus affect, and be affected by, each other and by the 'mind' of the universe, and should feel an urge to participate in the moulding of the world and in the forming of the 'decisions' to that end; it would indeed be surprising if it were not so, in some measure at any rate. The unity of all existence would appear to render that inevitable. The only real question is as to the extent to which such things do take place. Do they operate sufficiently for our consciousness to be aware of it? And experience answers that human consciousness is indeed aware of it. Prayer is one of the most deep-rooted and universal instincts of man; and telepathy is one of the experiences of which most people are convinced. Who is there who is not aware in his own mind of many such experiences of which he has no sort of doubt? For many people indeed prayer and telepathy are woven into the web and woof of life.

Scientific research has so far done little in this field; but it seems not improbable that we are on the threshold of significant advances in it.* Too much importance should not be attached to the paucity of the results so far obtained from what may be called laboratory tests for telepathy. Experience suggests that there are two conditions necessary to create the circumstances which are favourable for the occurrence of the phenomenon; first, there must be a strong bond of affection between the persons concerned, and second, the 'message' must be sent out under the stress of strong emotion. Both conditions are usually entirely lacking in set tests.

Prayer is a matter of the spirit. It is something we do within our minds. It consists of a conscious attuning of our spirits to the infinite universe, to God, who, as we have seen, must have all the attributes of personality, and a conscious effort to make our needs and desires known to Him and to enlist His aid in meeting them. It is no matter of words or language. Words, whether we use them within our own hearts or utter them aloud, or whether someone else utters them, are only of use as guides, helping to direct our minds into the appropriate channels and helping to induce the spirit of prayer.

People sometimes doubt the usefulness of prayer because they wonder how prayer, how an act of our spirits or wills, can have any influence on what happens in the world. But, in the first place, one of the main uses of prayer is not to influ-

* For an account of some comparatively recent advances in this sphere see *The Reach of the Mind* by J. B. Rhine, Director of the Parapsychology Laboratory of Duke University, U.S.A.

ence, or try to influence, anything that happens outside of ourselves at all. It is a means of readjusting and restoring our souls when they are troubled and tired and out of gear owing to the impacts of life; or of getting inner strength and guidance when difficulties loom ahead; or of just acquiring sufficient grace for the daily round. Sleep can attain similar results. How often have we wakened in the morning with a new outlook on life, or to find the solution of last night's baffling problem awaiting us in our minds? So it is with prayer. Given a few moments of real prayer, and our troubles and difficulties are found to have mysteriously vanished away when the time of testing comes. You may say that such experiences are due to auto-suggestion; but what's in a name? It explains nothing to give the experience a label. What is auto-suggestion? Whence come the forces which cause its effects? What does matter is that it does work. It is of small consequence whether you call it auto-suggestion or whether you call it prayer. But it is not surprising that when we consciously set our minds in touch with the great universe by reminding ourselves of our lot and part in it, and by trying to view everything in its true place in the infinite and eternal life of the universe, in a spirit of seeking support from it—in other words when we pray to God—it is not surprising that our spirits should be restored and our minds cleansed and that calm should invade our souls. It is only what the unity of all existence would lead us to expect.

And, in the second place, as regards the possibility of influencing matters outside ourselves, much may perhaps be achieved by the direct telepathic influence of our minds on the minds of others—by what one might call the broadcasting of one's desires and will. Much too may perhaps be achieved indirectly by evoking the influence of the universe, somewhat as the tiny influence of a feeble wireless radiation may be worked up and amplified by the electro-magnetic influences on which it is brought to bear in a receiving set.

And when one bears in mind the spiritual nature of the universe, when one keeps in view that mind and matter are of one stuff, and that the voluntary activities of our bodies are the result of the operation of our wills on the physical matter composing our bodies, who dare say that our spirits, our wills, may not have some direct influence, however slight, on physical things and happenings even outside ourselves?

Recent 'laboratory' tests indeed have disclosed that this is in fact the case.* And who dare say what the cumulative influence of the prayers of many may not do? But whatever the mechanics may be it does seem to work. Again and again, in matters small and great, those who pray have seen the apparent influence of their prayers. In such matters, it is true, it is hard to draw the line between coincidence and what is something more; but oft-repeated coincidence is what constitutes what we call 'law' in the physical world. And such apparent answers to prayer seem to occur too often, too regularly, and too obviously to be regarded always as mere coincidence. For many people they become part of the common technique and texture of life.

'But', you may ask, 'how can our prayers achieve anything when others may be praying for the exact opposite? Is one justified in asking God to do what others may equally desire and pray Him not to do?' Such questions are based on a wrong conception of prayer. Prayer does not seek to make use of God like a tool in man's hands. It is merely an expression of man's wants. The ultimate decision is left to God—to the judgment and will of the infinite universe. It is like the recording of a vote in a democratic form of government. As we are parts of the whole—citizens of the kingdom of heaven—it is our duty to take our share, however humble, in the framing of its 'policies' and 'decisions'. It is not for me to say I will not vote because one small vote can make so little difference or will be swamped by the deluge of votes of others to a contrary effect.

Or a better analogy perhaps is afforded by a nerve-cell in the human body. That nerve-end in your nose may urge you violently to scratch the tip of your nose; but there may be some very good reason known to you for refraining from responding—the sergeant-major on parade, for example! But the nerve-end would betray the very reason for its existence if if did not, with all that was in it, urge you to scratch. It is our duty as citizens of the kingdom of heaven, as members of the universal unity, in all things to make our requests known to God—and leave the rest to Him.

But our prayers have the best chance of achieving most the less they conflict with other influences, the more they are

* See *The Reach of the Mind, cit.*

73

in harmony with the whole universe—with God. Hence the value of bringing our prayers in imagination to the 'throne of God'. That raises in our minds a test of their worth and of their chances of success among the affairs of God's universe. We must put our spirits as fully as possible into harmony with the whole universe of God's creation before we can hope to pray to good effect.

> He prayeth well, who loveth well
> Both man and bird and beast.
>
> He prayeth best, who loveth best
>   All things both great and small;
> For the dear God who loveth us,
>   He made and loveth all.*

* *The Rime of the Ancient Mariner*—Samuel Taylor Coleridge.

XI. Religion

Prayer and religion are closely allied. Indeed it is difficult to say where the one ends and the other begins; but an essential element in religion is worship—loyalty to, and faith in, some being conceived as being greater than ourselves and greater than anything in the mere physical world. The highest forms of religion seek the object of worship in the Supreme Being, the ruler of all existence.

Like prayer, religion is one of the most deeply rooted and universal instincts of man. The churches, cathedrals, synagogues, mosques and temples which raise their arms to heaven in every corner of the Earth bear testimony to this. No one who neglects religion in some form or other can enjoy the fullest life. He is denying one of the cravings of his heart, just as he would if he neglected love and human relationships, or art, music, literature, painting, sculpture, architecture, the drama, or any of the many other things that enrich life. It is of course possible to exaggerate the importance of this or that element in life. If one would find the fullest joy in living, and so fulfil its purpose, one must have a well-balanced admixture of many interests. It is the spice of variety, the interplay of different interests, which constitutes the very essence of creative joy throughout the whole gamut of existence. One person may have a greater capacity for interests than another. But life without some form of religion is incomplete.

A man must be dead in soul and imagination if he is not stirred by a glorious sunset, a great landscape, or the star-spangled heavens, or by the marvels of science, or by achievements which reveal the wonders of the spirit of man. If there is any life in a man's soul such things evoke feelings which cannot be put into words, a feeling of awe, a yearning for we know not what, a sense of belonging to something vastly greater than anything we know—something to which these things belong so that they belong to us too—a sense of being ourselves something bigger, finer, greater than the being we present to the world and with which we busy ourselves in daily life. We do indeed in such experiences overstep the limits of space and time, and experience something of our real oneness with all existence. From such moments we emerge with a renewed sense of dignity and destiny, inspired with new hope, new courage, a new urge to live and achieve. It is such feelings, such experiences, which it is the function of religion to evoke. They are the upsurgings of faith.

It might well be asked why, in a world properly organised by Universal Being, in which man's life is set by Him with a definite purpose—why it should be necessary for man to pause from time to time from fulfilling his proper functions in order to evoke by artificial stimulation a sense of his place in the wider life of the universe outside the world in which God has set him. Animals and birds, fishes and trees, or a grain of mustard seed, feel no need for such exercises; and yet they are no doubt completely certain, without the slightest qualm of doubt, that they are fulfilling their destiny, fulfilling the purposes which Universal Being has set for them. The explanation lies in the difference between man and these 'lower' forms of life. If man had remained at a stage of evolution similar to the vegetables and the animals his life would run in grooves which God had prepared for him, guided unerringly by instincts acquired and shaped by the experience of countless ages handed on with the germ of life itself from generation to generation; and he would have no need for further guidance. But man's life did not remain at that level. God planted in man a creative urge so vigorous that it could not be denied; and so he finds himself now in a world largely of his own devising, a world in which he has no appropriate instincts to guide him, a world which hopelessly outstrips any possibility of such instincts developing in time to help him before he moves on to further developments, while many of the instincts he does have, inherited from his primordial past, would lead him the wrong way in this new world of his own creating. And so he tends to lose the way, and he tends moreover to get bogged down under the sheer weight of the things he himself has created.

He builds houses, for instance, and then has to devote much time to tending and maintaining them. He creates music and then has to spend much time making instruments and training musicians to produce it. He cultivates corn and then has to go on cultivating it because it has supplanted his natural sources of food. And so on through the whole sweep of civilisation. In his day-to-day constant striving with the materials out of which he has created his world man tends to become mere matter himself, to lose his own soul, his own will, his own dreams and ideals, and to become a mere cog in the machinery of civilisation.

And yet the very mainspring of the creative urge is the desire for joy, for change, for living more and more abundantly; and it can never be satisfied till it embraces all the joy and life that universal life can afford. And all the time, in responding to the urge, man is getting farther from the guidance of his instincts. And so he needs from time to time to pause and take stock and find his bearings anew, to find his proper setting in time and eternity, and to restore his soul. This is largely the theme of that ancient epic of the Creation and the birth of civilisation preserved for us in the Book of Genesis.

Ethics is not necessarily a concern of religion; but any worth-while vision of God must react on morals because of the sense of unity with all that exists which it must stimulate. Moreover the highest achievements of man whether in the moral or any other sphere are only attained under the influence of passionate devotion to some cause. Even in the ordinary affairs of daily life some aim is needed to achieve the best and to avoid pitfalls. An aimless life leads nowhere. There are many incentives which suffice for this or that sphere of life, but only religion affords a vital stimulus which embraces every sphere and aspect of life and conduct and human endeavour.

No doubt we can adjust and restore our spirits by communing with nature, by reading fine books, by losing ourselves in music, by private prayer, and in many other ways; but the practice of organised religion affords one of the best and readiest ways. There is virtue in the sense of belonging to a great movement actuated by a common faith. And religion never burns so strongly in the individual heart as when a number are gathered together seeking contact with the eternal verities in a joint act of religious observance. It is then that religious feelings are most readily evoked.

We can get in touch with the eternal verities; we can feel their impact; but we have no language in which we can readily communicate our thoughts and experiences about them to other people. We have a generally understood vocabulary only for the affairs of the every-day world in which we live—the world of space and time. And so, since religion is for the whole of mankind, the common run of unlettered people no less than the learned, the eternal verities have to be expressed in metaphors. We have no other language in which to express them in a way that all may understand. So for the most fundamental truths religion uses the simplest metaphors. The 'fatherhood' of God, the 'brotherhood' of man, for instance, are familiar and easily understood conceptions of every-day use in religion.

But it must never be forgotten that the language of religion is only metaphor. It must never be strained beyond its aptitude. That simple conception, for instance, that God is the Universal Father of man, with its corollary that man is the son of God, very aptly describes the ultimate reality of the relation between the Infinite, the Eternal, the Universal, and man. But it is only a metaphor and, like all metaphors, its appropriateness and validity break down if stretched too far. The terms 'father' and 'son', for instance, properly refer to a particular biological phenomenon in the propagation of the species which occurs in animals in general and in man in particular. But God is neither an animal nor a man. To apply these terms literally to the relation between God and man would be preposterous. So limited indeed is the appositeness of that metaphor that Christian doctrine uses the same metaphor to express an entirely different matter—to express what it regards as the unique relationship between God and Jesus. Christ is 'the son of God' in a sense quite different from that in which any man is. And so he is described as the 'only-begotten Son of God', and it has to be explained that he is a Son of God in a different sense than that in which any man is a son of God, and that God is his father in a different sense from that in which He is the father of any man. (Though this does not mean that every Christian accepts that distinction. There are Christians who like to think of Jesus as endowed with modesty, that crowning glory of the truly great, and who interpret the records as indicating that he himself claimed to be a 'son of God' only in respect of being a 'son of man'—the idiom for 'man' in the Aramaic language which he spoke.)

Translated into terms of the philosophic conceptions which we have been following in the previous chapters, the conception which these metaphors seek to put into words is that God expresses Himself, for men, more fully through man than through any other thing which He has created, and loves him more, but that He loves Jesus Christ so much more, and expresses Himself so much more fully through him than through any other man, that Christ expresses God in a sense which is exceptional and unique. And so it is with the other major doctrines of the Christian faith. They are not inconsistent with the philosophy enunciated in this book. The philosophy seeks to give them a fuller meaning.

So if we are inclined at times to think that the conceptions and language used in religion are crude and inadequate, or if they grate on our susceptibilities, it is useful to remind ourselves that they are only metaphors—that they only could be metaphors—and that they are metaphors chosen to suit the capacities of the humblest of ordinary people. And so it is with the rites and symbols of religious faiths. Men are so constituted that they need ceremonies and observations, signs and insignia and organisations, to hold them together. The little customs and ceremonies, for instance, which are so scrupulously observed in a battalion or in a military mess—little things like the way of saluting, the swing of the arms in marching, something in the uniform or in the way of wearing it, some bit of special etiquette—things which to an outsider may look meaningless or even silly but which have their origins in the history and traditions of the corps—these things have a definite value for the men who practise them, for their *esprit de corps*, for the morale of the regiment. Or these last words, that last message flashed from a post which had held out to the last man in some hard-fought battle—they have become a rallying-cry for the battalion. And so it is in religion.

A religious communion has a similar use for ceremonies and observances and forms of speech peculiar to itself and perhaps strange and uninspiring to others. Such things are the framework which gives religion its coherence and which focuses the loyalty of its adherents. We should not despise them when we do not understand them or cannot feel in harmony with them.

On the other hand we must not run away with the idea that any of the language or the phrases or the dogmas of religion, in so far as they purport to express eternal truths or ultimate realities, can be completely valid or sacrosanct. They are at best only metaphors or symbols, so that there can be no question of their ultimate validity but only of whether they are more adequate or less adequate to express the conceptions which they seek to enshrine. And even these very conceptions themselves are not sacrosanct. They are not the only, nor even necessarily the best, means of bringing home to the mind of man the things of infinity and eternity, the things of ultimate truth, which really matter to man.

We have seen how all the elements of life which we experience in our own minds are necessarily inherent in all existence. So it is valid to use any of them as something to which to relate all else, as something by which to describe or explain —something to express—any of the things of all existence, any of the things of God. One may describe the purposes and activities of God in terms of adventure, for instance, or of sacrifice, of overcoming sin or spiritual inertia, of seeking joy, of love, of suffering, of beauty, or of any of the other myriad ingredients of life and existence. They are all equally valid, provided they are not stressed beyond their due proportions in the make-up of universal existence. This, that, or the other of them may be the one which it is of the most service to stress at this or that juncture in the affairs of men. One religion may stress one, another religion another; but religion at its best should not be irrevocably tied to any. It should be free to use whichever is most needed for the guidance of man at the moment. It is a fatal error in religious matters to regard one particular mode of expression, one particular creed or set of dogmas, as the only valid one. It is deplorable to contemplate the strife and misery which have raged throughout man's history, mortally hindering his progress, over such blunders—the blunders of earnest people who could only see a portion of the truth at a time.

And thus has arisen throughout the ages the eternal conflict between prophet and priest, between poets, seers, preachers, those who seek to clothe the eternal truths in conceptions and language which will inspire the world to new life, hope, and energy, on the one hand and those who seek to preserve all that is good and useful to man in the conceptions, the language, and traditions of the past, on the other hand. Nor is the conflict always between different people. It is often a conflict within the heart and mind of one and the same person. Indeed what the needs of man demand is a due balance between these two tendencies, at one time yielding preference to the one, at another to the other, according to the circumstances of the time, so that the eternal truths may always be presented to men in a way which they can understand. But at epochs in the affairs of men there come times when the need for restatement of the fundamental truths has far outstripped the need to preserve the achievements of the past. Religion at such times may have become formal and dead, bogged down perhaps in tradition; and it urgently needs to be stirred into new life by being given new expression with a vital meaning and purpose for the new day and generation. And so often the need produces the man. A prophet arises and proclaims the eternal truths in a new language, the language of his own day, the language of the people and of common-sense which all can understand. And there follows a revival in religion and the life of the time.

It is not that the fundamental truths, the eternal verities, have been changed. They have only been presented in a form appropriate to the time. They are like wine. Each new year's crop produces a new vintage, with its own peculiar characteristics, but it is always wine, the fruit of the grape. And—to borrow a metaphor from the days when wine-bottles were of skin—you cannot put new wine in old bottles. New religious conceptions and forms must be found which will contain the new expression, the new revelation, of the unchanging truth. 'God is a spirit, and they that worship Him must worship Him in spirit and in truth.'

Our Lord was a supreme and daring exponent of this method, in startling contrast to the scribes and pharisees, the theologians of his time, who clung slavishly to the words of the ancient sacred writings. And he had hardly departed before St. Paul, another great exponent of the method, was already recasting Jesus' message. And he did it so thoroughly that he shocked and puzzled some of his Jewish fellow-apostles; and even to this day there are those who think that he promulgated a new religion altogether—Paulinism, as distinct from the gospel which Jesus preached.

The present times seems to be one of those epochs when the language of religion has lagged too far behind the language in current use. Concepts which were adequate to convey the eternal truths with which religion is concerned two thousand years ago, because these concepts were vital realities then in the every-day life of men, are quite inadequate today because they hold no vital meaning in our present-day world. Such for instance are the conceptions of the Christian faith associated with the Jewish sacrificial rites. These conceptions were largely designed by the early Christian apostles to sweep away all the hampering preoccupation of contemporary Jews with the exacting ritual demands of the Jewish religious code, which intruded at every turn in their daily life. These Christian apostles reckoned that all this slavery to a code, 'the law', had to be got rid of in one way or another so that the Jews could make a fresh start with the gospel of living by love which Jesus preached. And it was easier to introduce this new doctrine of a final and complete sacrificial fulfilment of 'the law' than to displace the orthodox Jew's belief in the sacredness of 'the law'. But to twentieth-century man, outside the Jewish community at any rate, these rites mean nothing unless they are explained to him; and so they fail, without explanation, to convey the truth they were employed by the early Christians to convey to their Jewish compatriots. Indeed twentieth-century man feels little of any such sense of guilt, any such sense of obligations unfulfilled and impending awful retribution in consequence. Aspiration dominates his attitude to life rather than fear. Having put his hand to the plough he does not look back.

Our Earth is no longer thought of as the hub of the universe and the reason for its existence, but as a minor satellite of a very minor star—a tiny speck in a vast universe of universes. This is the age of electricity, of radio-activity, of atomic energy, of space probing, of 'wireless' and television, of harnessing nature to man's uses, of engines, motors, and machinery, of the electro-magnetic theory of matter, of psychology, of scientific discipline applied to theory and research, and of a host of other things and conceptions which were unknown even fifty or a hundred years ago, let alone two thousand years ago. Many conceptions of a hundred or even fifty years ago are outmoded now for the purpose of conveying fundamental truths. The modes of thought, the pre-occupations of man, have so completely changed. As well offer mediaeval charts to the navigator of an aeroplane—although the basic principles of navigation have not changed; but it would be futile to try to describe them today in terms of the conceptions which were found adequate two thousand years ago. Such old-world things have their uses. They need not be completely discarded. They should be put away in the armoury or the treasure-store, to be brought out as occasion may require or to form the basis of some treasured tradition or some hallowed rite.

XII. Debunking Life

Who that reads current fiction has not come across the type of novel which debunks life? The characters seem to give unrestricted play to animal instinct. The author seems to believe that he is depicting normal people. He makes no sort of apology for them. Indeed he may even sneer at the 'inhibitions' and 'repressions' of people who do control their natural instincts, and suggest that such restraint is likely to induce mental disorder or that it is 'bourgeois', the stamp of inferior class. And he depicts love in terms of sex-instinct, and sex-instinct itself as just a device of nature for the perpetuation of the species, and dismisses all deeper feelings as mawkish sentiment.

Such books leave one with an impression of life as a sordid affair in which man lives in the grip of soulless nature with little power of control over his own life and destiny. The Marxist theory of dialectical materialism has something of the same sort in it, as it is applied to the history and development of human affairs, in its assumption that they are completely controlled by natural laws.

It is indeed small wonder that time and again man falls into sin. His whole body, with all its mental and psychological make-up and all its inherited instincts, was designed for a different kind of life altogether from that which civilised man has built up for himself. It was designed for life in the jungle. All his more or less civilised experience since his jungle days has made little change in his physical make-up and instincts. Evolution, however it works, lags far behind the remotest possibility of catching up with the changes man works in his own environment.

And so man has this wonderful instrument, the human body, put into his hands with which to create his own life; but it is designed for quite a different purpose; and if he is indeed to create his own life, if he is to use this instrument instead of allowing it to use him, then he must needs keep it under firm control. It is like taming a wild animal, like breaking in a horse, and using it for one's own purposes. But to control a horse is easier. Its controller is in a detached position. The horse's instincts affect itself alone, not its rider. Man's physical instincts affect the very mind which seeks to control them, threatening at times to engulf that mind in their flood.

Early training and education, the moral sense, the restraints imposed by society, all greatly aid us in managing our physical beings; but it is small wonder that times without number the animal in us gets some of its own way, and that it sometimes takes the bit between its teeth and bolts. That is what makes human tragedy. But most people who can be classed as humans have their animal natures under sufficient control most of the time. Otherwise civilisation would disappear.

Nor is it surprising that the strain of the conflict proves too much for some people and results in mental illness of one sort or another. But that does not mean that the whole endeavour should be abandoned by mankind. There are soldiers who fall out on a route march, and some who prove altogether unfit for the strain; but that does not mean that it is too great a strain for men in general and that route marches and military training should therefore be abandoned. It only means that the medical officer must deal with the men who fall out. And so it is the function of psychology to unravel all it can of the mysteries of the working of the human mind in order to help us most effectively to control and use our physical make-up for our own ends. And it is a function of medical science, including psychiatry, to use the discoveries of psychology to aid in the diagnosis and treatment of the casualties in the fight of the human mind over the jungle—the fight for civilisation.

But that does not mean that we all suffer from the disabilities and weaknesses which cause the casualties. For most of us the strain of the necessary 'repressions' is well within our capacity; and the casualties afford us no excuse for slacking. That way lies the jungle. Every part of the civilised world which man has created for himself is based on the control and direction of natural laws and instincts into new directions of man's own choosing. If the barriers and restraints were broken down that would be the end of civilisation.

It is a trite saying that life is full of paradoxes. There is for instance the fact that the more one chases after happiness the more it eludes one. Another such is that the more one consciously strives to cure one's moral failings the less likely is one to lose them. The more one occupies oneself with repenting of them, with thinking about them, with resisting their lure, the more one becomes enmeshed in them, and the less likely are they to be cured. It is very important to take a good hard look at our faults sometimes; but if we linger too long over the process, if we give our faults undue importance, then when we have driven out the evil thing for the moment, and swept and garnished our souls, it returns by and by in renewed strength, or other evil things come, to fill the emptiness; and our last state is worse than our first. The sovereign remedy for sin is to forget it in some other absorbing interest, worthy in itself, which claims our whole-hearted attention; or in some passionate devotion which grips our whole being; or maybe just in loyalty to the community in which our lot is cast. And then we will find by and by that the power of our sin has vanished away unawares.

The rider would never gain complete mastery over the horse if he did not forget the routine business of control in anticipation of what he can achieve when the horse is at his command. And man could never master the animal within him unless he forgot the discipline and repression in the desire for what civilisation offers.

Herein lies the sinister influence of the kind of writing which 'debunks' life. Quite apart from the perilous ease of rousing the baser passions, man needs to have before him an alluring picture of life, and to believe in it, to believe in its worth-whileness and in the possibility of attaining it, if he is to rise to the effort which alone can make the great adventure of civilisation succeed. It is merely playing with words to say that art is not concerned with morality, that the function of the novelist or the dramatist is to depict life as it is, not as it should be. Nothing that man does or creates is in itself concerned with morality. It is the use that he makes of it that is. The surgeon's art is not in itself concerned with morality; but if it were turned to murder it would be. If writings so skilfully play on a man's feelings as to incite him to murder they are criminal, and no juggling with words about the sacredness of art can make them otherwise. Neither can the writers of fiction which by debunking life incites to licence, to the loosening of human ties, to lower ways of life, to mere indulgence, escape moral responsibility.

This calls for no prudery, nor does it call for the shutting of one's eyes to the realities of life and human nature as it is. Shakespeare is an outstanding example of creative genius combined with a sense of moral responsibility. His plays evade none of the wickedness, the weakness of mankind; and yet to see them or to read them is an ennobling experience.

The love-passion of a man and a woman is no doubt a device of nature for the perpetuation of the species. That is a perfectly valid statement from one point of view. Everything that is worth while in life could probably be similarly regarded as a device of nature for some purpose or other—probably of less use, if any use at all, in our present-day life. And if that were the whole story everything in life could be debunked, and life made to look like an arid and futile jest cynically perpetrated upon us by nature.

That wonderful sunset, for instance, which floods your soul with unutterable emotions—why should a mere arrangement of colours so entrance you? If you could probe far enough into your subconscious self you would find some quite prosaic reason. Probably, like the appendix, it is merely a hang-over from some far back stage in evolution—perhaps a relic of the instinct which allures an insect to the bright colours of a flower—another device of nature for a utilitarian end.

What can we gain by just seeing our friends and those we love? What do we gain by just having them around, engaging perhaps in quite trivial conversation, or none at all, and doing nothing whatever of a practical nature for each other? And yet some of the most profound and lasting joys of life consist in just that. The pleasure it gives is probably associated with some remnants of the herd instinct, which did serve a practical purpose in a primordial past. But who cares about the why? All that matters to us is that it does give us pleasure.

Psychology may some day be able to trace the origins of all the things that make life seem worth while. But all that psychology or any other science can do in the matter is to throw light on how our minds work. It can unravel the intricacies and complexities of the mind's machinery, and so it can help us to use our mental and psychological make-up to better advantage, and to treat those whose frail constitutions have broken down under the strain of civilised life. But it can tell us nothing at all about ultimate realities. It cannot tell us what mind is, why it should have any machinery at all, what is life, what the existence is with which these things are concerned or what is the meaning or purpose of any of it.

All our emotions are doubtless an inheritance from the dim, remote, past—the jungle out of which man has evolved. Indeed our whole physical make-up is just an inheritance. But for the man who truly is a man it is of small consequence how these things originated. They are all just the raw materials out of which he fashions his own world. They are the bricks and mortar with which he builds his own spiritual home, the marble which he shapes to express the creations of his own soul.

What, for instance, can be the pleasure of placing pieces of printed cardboard on a table in a certain sequence? Yet man has used the ordinary human instincts and emotions to turn just such things into fascinating pastimes and games, which he himself has created together with all their elaborate rules. Such is bridge; such is chess; and such are the countless other sports and pastimes with which man fills so much of his life. And so it is also in the more serious affairs of life. Man has turned all his inherited instincts and emotions to his own uses.

Every man must sooner or later make up his mind whether he is going to use these materials provided by nature or is going to allow them to use him—whether he is going to be a man or just a cog in the machinery of nature. If he decides to be master and use them, then it is for him a second birth, the birth of the spirit. It opens the way to life on a new plane.

But he must face the issues. It involves self-sacrifice. For it involves the abandonment among other things of the free play of his natural instincts. It involves their control by his will—in order to attain the new worlds which man can create, in order to achieve civilisation, to enter the kingdom of heaven.

He needs to decide too whether he is going to try to

usurp the benefits of civilisation, which other people have won for him, without paying the price in self-control and obedience to the code of conduct on which the civilisation depends. And he needs constantly to face these issues anew at each fresh turn of life.

XIII. Genesis

The account of the beginnings of the world and of man and of civilisation which forms the first three chapters of our Bible provides a fascinating commentary on the matters which we have been discussing in this book, culled from ancient times and conceived in poetic vein.

The interpretation of Genesis which sees in it only something that is intended to be a factual account of these matters stultifies it completely. The charmingly naïve interpretation indeed which would see in it a statement that the world and everything in it were created in a period of six days of twenty-four hours each, and by a series of instantaneous acts of creation, is self-evidently devoid of any real foundation in Genesis itself.

It is plain for instance from the narrative that the word 'day', as used throughout the English Authorised Version in these passages, is not used in the sense of an astronomical day, or twenty-four hours, but like the Hebrew word in the original text as a period of time, an epoch—as when we say, for instance, 'in my grandfather's day', or 'the day of the bow and arrow'.

In one place (Chap. II, v. 4), for instance, the word is used to denote the whole period of six days of the creation, and in another (Chap. I, v. 5) it is used as meaning light as distinct from darkness (before astronomical day and night had come into existence); and 'the evening and the morning', which constitutes each of the 'days' of creation is no way of describing the astronomical day of morning, noon, evening and night of every-day occurrence. And the happenings on the sixth 'day', described in another place (Chap. II, from v. 19) could not by the wildest stretch of imagination take place within the span of one day of twenty-four hours or indeed of myriads of such days. They would take at least hundreds of years to accomplish. Indeed they seem altogether impossible for one man (the naming of every creature) and Adam was alone at that time. Eve was not created till later on that 'day' —an event which in itself, as described, would occupy a good part, if not the whole, of a day. In our communings with God no language is needed; but what language could there be for Adam to use to name the creatures when there was as yet no one for him to talk to? Doubtless with God all things are possible. The natural laws which He made He could equally over-rule. But the fact that the author of Genesis narrates these naturally fantastically impossible happenings for one 'day' without comment or explanation shows that it simply did not occur to him that anyone could imagine his 'day' was other than an epoch.

Moreover at the beginning of the 'week' of creation space and time did not exist. Their existence could not be imposed on God as that would imply some superior being to do so; and so He would not be God at all. Time and space, like everything else in heaven and earth according to this account, were created by God, and at the beginning of the process of creation they did not exist at all. The author of Genesis recognises this. 'The earth was without form and void.' And time in our sense, of astronomically measured duration, or a day of twenty-four hours, could not come into being until the fourth 'day' with the creation of the sun and stars.

And—to go to the other end of the 'week' of creation, the seventh 'day', the 'day' in which God rested from creating new things—it has already, on the lowest computation, lasted nearly six thousand years and will presumably last as long as this world lasts. But of the actual length of any of these 'days' or epochs Genesis tells us nothing.

The narrative shows everything in heaven and earth as created and existing by God's will alone; but except in one instance it is silent as to whether He created them by a series of instantaneous acts or by a process of gradual development or evolution, and as to whether in the process He made use of the natural processes He had already created such as gravitation, natural selection, or any other. But it is significant that in the only case where any details of the process are given, the creation of Eve, it is depicted as by no means an instantaneous process, but a somewhat prolonged and elaborate one, making full use of the natural world and processes which He had already created.

It is difficult however to understand how anyone can read these chapters of Genesis without becoming aware that what he is reading does not purport to be a factual account of anything, but, like the Psalms of David or the Song of Solomon, is poetry, an epic poem (or poems) whose theme, portrayed with majestic imagery and masterly grasp, is man's place in God's universe and the consequences for man of his having taken the ordering of his life into his own hands and broken away from the dominion of natural law—natural law which God had created—in the shape of natural instinct—the consequences moral, spiritual, social and economic.

That it was natural law that was concerned is signified by the fact that the break-away occurred over a matter of diet, in which no ethical issues were involved. And the consequence depicted are just those which in fact, within human experience, have always resulted from man's efforts in controlling natural forces and natural laws and instincts for his own ends instead of blindly submitting to them like the animals—when he has launched out into an artificial, a civilised, way of life. And Genesis also recognises the complexity of the consequences owing to the circumstance that it was God Himself who not only created man but also put into him the creative urge which led him to try to break away from natural law. 'God . . . breathed into his nostrils the breath of life: and man became a living soul.' This is a reflection of the paradox at the core of all existence.

For Christians the supreme importance of Genesis is that it enshrines the very kernel of the gospel. It shows man, like everything else, as created by God and as continuing to exist only by God's will, but as expressing God more articulately than any of His other creations. 'God created man in His own image' (Chap. I, 26, 27) and charged him with the duty of carrying on the work of creation in the world (Chap. I, v. 28).

XIV. The Gospel According to Jesus

It is unfortunate that the records we have of the teachings of Jesus are so fragmentary and obscure. They lend themselves in consequence to a great variety of interpretation. The history of the Christian religion bears tragic testimony to this. When one reads the records against the background of the philosophy developed in the preceding chapters of this book, some new light appears to be thrown on the Gospel of Jesus, and yet another interpretation seems to emerge. The following are some reflections suggested by such a reappraisal of the records contained in the four Gospels.

It must be reiterated that all the conceptions of theology are only symbols and metaphors. They are intended to depict ultimate things for which we have no other language which people in general could understand. For instance, if one may add to the illustrations already referred to, one of the central conceptions of the Christian faith is that God once came to this Earth and lived for some years in it (in the person of our Lord Jesus Christ). But then God is everywhere all the time. This physical universe exists only by His will, in His mind. So even by physical standards God must be bigger than the whole physical universe. Taken literally, it would be altogether meaningless to talk of God coming to the Earth and living in it. It would have as little meaning as it would to talk of the Earth coming to one of the atoms which constitute its own substance and joining in the stream of electrons round its nucleus. Only it would be incomparably more nonsensical to talk of God coming to the Earth. The conception is only a metaphor—a metaphor designed to try to convey some idea of the very special relation which the Christian faith recognises between God and our Lord.

And so it is with all the conceptions of theology. They must perforce be expressed in metaphor, in word-pictures or cartoons, if they are to be intelligible to ordinary people. What ideas they raise in the minds of those to whom they are addressed depends on their habits of thought, their current beliefs, their mode of life, their environment. Metaphors are used which seem apt for the day and generation to whom they are addressed; but we must never forget that they are nothing more than metaphors.

Conventional Christian belief is surrounded by a halo of religious emotion which is apt to blur the perception of its devotees. It comprises many conceptions of great beauty. Taken separately, they are adequate enough to express the particular aspects of the faith to which they relate—for people at any rate who have been reared in that theological tradition. But it is full of inconsistencies and mutual contradictions which are either glossed over as mysteries or just ignored. Looking at it steadily and whole, however, as in the end one must if one is to have a steadfast faith, and as ordinary people not versed in its technicalities inevitably do, it breaks down. When viewed whole, its effect is to represent this universe as governed by a sadistic spirit who has created it in order to gratify his appetite for inflicting pain. It represents man as doomed by his 'fall' to eternal torture in hell by God's decree; and yet it was God who created man and made him what he is; and God moreover specifically breathed into him the breath of life, planted in him the creative urge which was bound sooner or later to lead him into just such an enterprise of originality as that which is said to have constituted his 'fall'; moreover it can only have been God Himself who made the law by which such conduct on man's part was something wrong. God, the Omnipotent, could not be subject to any law but His own will. To get over this logical impasse, another agent, the devil, is introduced to try to account for man's 'fall' in a way that does not involve God in responsibility for it. It is the devil, it is said, who lured man thus to destruction. But God created everything in heaven and earth, in all existence; there is nothing in heaven or earth that was not created by God; so, if there is a devil, God must have created the devil also. Indeed the devil is acknowledged to be one of the 'sons of God' (Job, I, 6). So that in the last resort God is solely responsible for the whole set-up of world, man, law, devil, and hell. They were all created by His will alone, and continue to exist by His will alone, and for His good pleasure. He could have made them in any form He chose, but He chose that particular form.

God is also represented as having told man at an early stage in his history that his 'fall' had thus doomed him to eternal torture, but that he could escape that fate if he strictly observed certain rules* and religious rites, including the offering of sacrifices to atone for any lapse from the strict code, and provided he belonged to a certain small chosen race. The rest of mankind were foredoomed to torture. Even the chosen people were left in agonising doubt till their very last moment on Earth in case they had failed in some particular of the code (the 'Law').

Then God is represented as having, at a later stage, sent His dearest treasure, His son, into the Earth in the guise of a man, Jesus Christ our Lord, and as having subjected him to untold spiritual suffering and physical torture in order to gratify His craving to make man suffer for his 'fall', and in order to absolve man from the punishment of eternal torture to which He Himself, entirely of His own will, had previously condemned man—a picture, if ever there was one, of shameless, exquisite, sadism.

But this by no means meant that mankind were really reprieved. It is true the condition that one must belong to the chosen race was waived; but it was only those select few who really believed this story about the sacrifice of God's Son who were reprieved, and only then provided they observed certain parts of the old code and in addition certain new rules and rites, and (according to some theologians) provided also that they were members of a particular community or sect or church. The rest of mankind, incalculably the greater part, remain under God's condemnation. And even the select few must remain in agonising uncertainty till the very end—do they in their inmost hearts really believe that story? Does God, who sees into the innermost secrets of one's being, perceive their traces of unbelief? Have they perchance failed in some particular of what is required by the code? And on top of all

---

* The rules included some of an ethical nature; but God was not supposed to be concerned with ethics, only with the code as such—what He had decreed. Jesus pointed out that, on the contrary, God is not really concerned with any code, as such, but only with morals.

this there is the doctrine propounded by some Christians that it is not anything which they themselves do which decides their salvation (from eternal torture) but something which God does to them, and only if He chooses them for the purpose. And the only way one knows if one is one of the elect is by having undergone a particular spiritual and emotional experience called 'conversion'. Has he really experienced this? Is any experience he has had really 'conversion'? To the very end one must remain in torturing uncertainty. And this forsooth, in one of its forms or another, is the gospel, the 'glad tidings' of God's wonderful grace towards men!

What a relief it is to turn from all this to the gospel as propounded by our Lord himself! He committed none of it to writing. It has been handed down to us through many hands and many translations and re-translations. His original reporters probably did not fully understand all he said, and coloured it with their own ideas and prejudices, as people do in such circumstances. The narrative as we have it today also contains many obvious additions made, consciously or unconsciously, by the various transcribers. And naturally Jesus explained his gospel in terms of the idiom of his day, in terms of the conventions and modes of thought and belief, the language and history and environment, in which his hearers lived and which they could understand, and in stories which would have a dramatic impact on their minds. And so to us much of what he is reported to have said seems obscure; but the essentials of his gospel seem to stand out clearly from the narrative. There is a marked absence in it of the kind of inconsistency and mystery to which we have been referring. There is mystery indeed in abundance in everything in this world, in everything in the whole vast universe; but there appears to be nothing more of mystery in the gospel as our Lord explained it than in any of the ordinary things of daily life. Indeed his gospel appears to be based on sound down-to-earth common-sense.

Reading the narrative in the light of these considerations, Jesus appeared to be at pains to make it clear that when he spoke of the kingdom of heaven he was not referring to something which is primarily concerned with life beyond the grave but to something which, though it is concerned with life in all eternity, is primarily concerned with this present life, here and now ('The kingdom of heaven is at hand'). It is concerned with the ordinary things that fill our lives, such as the pleasure we get from children ('Of such is the kingdom of heaven.') It is not concerned with trying to win God's favour but with things which we value for their own sakes, without any ulterior aims, as children are absorbed in their own entrancing occupations ('Ye must become as little children'). It is concerned with the sort of things we value above all else, like a priceless pearl which someone might prize so much that he would be ready to sacrifice everything else to possess it. It is in fact the realm of pure delight. The kingdom of heaven is not something which gives us gladness of heart. It is the gladness of heart itself. For gladness of heart is the sign and seal of God's approval. It is the true aim of all things created by God and into which He has breathed His breath of life ('The kingdom of heaven is within you'). And, said Jesus, God does not grudge it to us. It is what He plans for us. It is His good pleasure to give it to us (Luke XII, 32).

In short the gospel which our Lord preached was not the secret of how to escape from the vengeance of an exacting deity, how to escape the terrors of some hell beyond the grave. It was the prescription for achieving abundant life, joy without limit, here and now and always, in time and eternity. Notwithstanding some of the illustrations he used to thrust home his points, it was not to fear that he appealed but to aspiration.

And what was his prescription? When challenged to state it clearly, he said the whole of it from beginning to end was contained in a few well-known words from the Old Testament; that his gospel consisted in the proper understanding of that gem: 'Thou shalt love the Lord thy God with all thy Heart, and with all thy soul, and with all thy strength, and with all thy mind; this is the first great commandment. And the second is like unto it. Thou shalt love thy neighbour as thyself. On these two commandments hang all the law and the prophets. This do, and thou shalt live' (Deut. VI, 5; Lev. XIX, 18; Matt. XXII, 37, 38; Mark XII, 28–31; Luke X, 25–28).

It is astonishing that the Christian Churches pay so little regard to this pronouncement. Our Lord has expressly put his whole gospel thus in a nutshell, and has told us plainly that the whole message of the Bible is contained in it; but the Churches apparently prefer to put forward some elaborate creed or confession of faith. They may spare a passing nod for it, it is true, but if they do they almost invariably emasculate it by implying that it only means that one should obey certain commandments, should love the rites and services of the church and private devotions and religious observances, and should be charitable—this, forsooth, 'loving God with all our heart and soul and strength and mind'! That may have been how the injunction was interpreted in the pre-Christian era; but the essence of Jesus' teaching is to point out how vastly more is required by it.

How *can* one love God—God whom we have not seen? There is only one possible way—by loving the expression of Himself which God has chosen to give us—the world, the universe, in which we live. It is all an expression of God, its creator. It is how God has chosen to express Himself to us. It is the only way He does express Himself to us, apart from the vague and uncertain conceptions of Ultimate Realities which we find in our own hearts and minds. No doubt He puts these ideas into our minds too, or into the minds of inspired men; but if it were only these that we loved it would be not God we loved but only an image of God which we ourselves or other men have created, with, or perhaps without, some help from God prompting our thought. We would thus be preferring our own notion of what God should be to the way in which God Himself has chosen to present Himself to us. And, how- ever inspiration may work, it cannot afford a millionth part of the definiteness and fullness of God's revelation of Himself in His creation.

One can imagine our Lord saying 'If a man say I love God and loveth not the world which God has created, he is a liar; for he that loveth not the world which he has seen, how can he love God, its creator, whom he has not seen?' And, as a corollary, 'He that loveth not his brother whom God created in His own image, and whom he has seen, how can he love God whom he hath not seen? For God created this world with such infinitely loving care, and found it all so good, that He crowned it with the fullest expression of Himself that He has yet given—man, created in His own image, in the very like- ness of God.' And one can imagine the writer of the Epistle of John hearing him saying such things and later borrowing from his memory of them to reinforce his message of love (cf. John IV, 20, 21).

What then is the first and great commandment, the prescription for abundant life and joy without limit? In what way does our Lord's interpretation of this injunction differ from that of pre-Christian times? It is that one must first of all be in love with life and with all that it offers—must passionately love this world, this universe, and all that it contains, and must align oneself with God's work of creation in it—ally oneself with God, seeking with Him the success of His great adventure in creating it, as if it were our own father's domain to which one day we would succeed. No half-hearted devotion will do. It is not a matter of devoting oneself primarily to religion, to 'spiritual' things, and then being permitted to give some attention to 'worldly' affairs—which is how the Churches usually put it. It is the other way round. We are to devote our 'all', our whole being without reservation, all our heart and all our soul and all our strength and all our mind—we are to make it the aim and object of our lives—to further the world which God has created and all the affairs of mankind, the world's work and the world's play, to strive to shape it into something ever more worth while—although we are permitted, because of our weakness, to seek comfort and strength in religion to help us to do so.

And if we do that, it follows as the night the day that we will love that part of God's universe which consists of other people and their lives, and will have their interests as close to our hearts as our own.

And that was just how Jesus himself lived, how he carried out this philosophy for living, in the circumstances and practical needs of his fellow-countrymen, crushed and humiliated by Rome.

But one cannot attain these joys to the full by just going through the motions of obeying the rules. It is no use doing the exercises for the sake of the benefits we may obtain, in order to achieve gladness of heart. Nature cannot be deceived. God is not mocked. There is no doubt some satisfaction to be had even in outward conformity to that way of life; but to enjoy the full satisfaction, these principles must be pursued for their own sake, with utter sincerity, without any ulterior motive, just because one loves to do so. This involves a particular orientation of one's whole being. It is an attitude which does not come naturally. It involves a fundamental change, a complete re-orientation—what Jesus graphically described as a second birth, an awakening of the spirit (see John III, 1–21).

That may seem an impossible task to set a man. Love is something we cannot create to order. We either love a person or a thing or we do not. If love does not come naturally we cannot force it, we cannot create it in our hearts. Only the Creator of all things, who made us as we are, can do that. And so we are unable of ourselves to bring about this complete transformation of our attitude to life. But, said Jesus, if we truly and humbly seek it, God will not fail to instil into our hearts the grace of an all-embracing love. ('. . . how much more shall your heavenly Father give the Holy Spirit to them that ask Him?' (Luke XI, 13). 'When he was yet a long way off his father saw him, and had compassion, and ran, and fell on his neck, and kissed him' (Luke XV, 20).) It is common experience, one of the facts of nature, that we come to love the people and things around us, the things in which we take an interest. If we interest ourselves in the world nature meets us halfway. It soon makes its fascination felt.

And if we fail to achieve this what is the penalty? It is not some dire punishment in a life beyond the grave. We may well be handicapped in some after life by not having lived aright in this life, just as we are in this one; but we know nothing about that. God has deliberately hidden such things from us. It is as though God—the Great Universe—had told us to leave all that to Him and to mind our own business, which is to live this life. It is no use pretending our hearts are glad when they are not; and it is what happens in our hearts that ultimately matters; that is where the kingdom of heaven, the bliss, exists or does not exist. That is the penalty if we fail to follow these simple rules of life. We fail to achieve all the gladness, all the satisfaction, that life offers us. It is a penalty which follows inevitably and which we cannot conceal from God, from nature, or from ourselves.

Some theology there must be in any worth-while religion, however simple. There must for instance be some conceptions about God and about God's relations with the world and with man. And however simple the faith, sooner or later the theology has to be elaborated by pursuing its implications into all the intricacies of life. This takes one into regions of thought, bordering on the infinite and eternal, where there are no land-marks, because they are beyond common human experience. So to aid in keeping our thoughts coherent we invent imagery, reference-frames consisting of apt metaphors and symbols, just as we invent a framework of imaginary lines of latitude and longitude to help us in navigation, geography, and astronomy. And thus a theology is evolved.

Our Lord has left no records of any elaborate scheme of theology; but from what he said about the law and the prophets hanging on these two commandments and about our having life if we conform to them, it is clear that his theology did not envisage any conception about our salvation being dependent on belief in any story about God sacrificing His son to atone for man's sin, or on observance of any rites or sacraments, or on belonging to any particular community or Church. And this is made even plainer by the 'Lord's Prayer', the prayer which our Lord gave to his disciples as a model of what prayer should be. If anything reflects a person's theology his prayers do. Jesus' prayer does not begin 'Father of our Lord Jesus Christ', but 'Our Father'—'your father and my father', as he said on other occasions. And it asks God to forgive us our trespasses, not because we believe in anything nor because we observe any rites or belong to any community, but 'as we forgive them that trespass against us'—in other words, because, like the Good Samaritan, we live by love.

No one can read the New Testament with a clear and open mind without observing that it appears to contain two distinct gospels—the gospel *of* our Lord and the gospel *about* our Lord. There is, on the one hand, the gospel which our Lord preached and explained and lived and which he finally died to further, which is concerned with mankind, with how man can achieve abundant life and unlimited joy, and which is chiefly contained in the four 'Gospels'. On the other hand, there is the gospel *about* our Lord, concerned with his place in God's plans and with the formation of a church, and which was first promulgated after our Lord's death, chiefly by St. Paul, and which is hardly if at all to be found in the four Gospels but is almost entirely confined to the other books of the New Testament.

The former, the gospel *of* our Lord, transcends all religion. The latter, the gospel *about* our Lord, represents the first attempts to enshrine the gospel of our Lord in a systematic theology, and in some kind of religious symbolism and organisation. It appears to have been inspired by the desire to commend his gospel to the day and generation of the early Church. Apart from the different content and quality of its faith, it tended to invest Christianity in the outward garb of just another religion. It was indeed very much on the lines of classical mythology. It was the basis from which all the generally accepted Christian theologies were evolved. Its metaphors may have been apt enough in the early centuries of the Christian Church, but they have long since lost their aptitude to depict the ultimate things, the eternal truths, they were intended to express.

No doubt there are many Christians who, if asked on a formal occasion, such as when being admitted to the membership of the church or presenting their baby for baptism, if they believe the conceptions of current Christian theology, would say without hesitation and without conscious dissimulation that they do. They have been familiar with its formulae all their lives, in school, catechism, creeds, and worship; so that they have become accustomed to them as the appropriate way of expressing their faith. But that, deep down in their consciousness, few if any professing Christians really accept these conceptions as adequately expressing their faith is disclosed in a simple way.

If any of them saw a friend straying unconsciously towards the edge of a dangerous precipice, they would, in their anxiety, shout warnings and seek urgently to avert a catastrophy. And if they saw their friend disappear over the edge their souls would be torn with anguish at the thought of what their friend would be suffering, assuming he had not been killed outright. They would be in no doubt as to the consequences of falling over the precipice. But when the same professing Christians see an unbelieving friend wandering in supposed danger, not of temporary suffering, but of eternal torture because of his unbelief, they take it quite calmly and do little if anything to avert the tragedy. And if death overtakes their friend and so, according to their professed beliefs, the friend has already begun to suffer the unspeakable pains of God's never-ending punishment, they give no thought to any such consideration. Their only concern is their grief at having lost their friend; because, deep down in their consciousness, they recognise that these theological conceptions are for them, quite devoid of any reality. And this accounts too for most of their reluctance to talk about their faith. It is because the conventional ways of expressing it ring false to themselves. They are all too conscious of the flagrant inaptness of the conventional forms to express their profound convictions. And they cannot find any other language to express it. Even the word 'God' they are chary of using because it has acquired so many associations of a crude and distasteful nature.

The ordinary man in the pew indeed looks on theology with a sort of amused indulgence as an intellectual pastime in which clerics and professors like to indulge by studying problems, and (like Job and his 'comforters') tying themselves in knots of their own creating, much as chess and bridge enthusiasts do with the intricacies of their games. But the clerical preoccupation with such matters cannot dim the gospel of the realm of bliss, the gospel of our Lord, which is what the occupants of the pew, deep down in their hearts, believe in and love.

As for the churchless masses, whom it should be the Church's most urgent task to evangelise, when the gospel is presented to them in terms of the traditional theology they find it either meaningless or simply repellent. It may have been well enough for the half thoughts of an unscientific age, but to twentieth-century man it savours of insult both to the Almighty and to their own intelligence, unless indeed he has been trained from infancy to appreciate its undoubted, if hidden, beauty. That is one of the main reasons why evangelistic campaigns so often fail to reach the masses, and why the impact of such campaigns tends to be so evanescent even on those who were already familiar with Christian teaching. Their new-found faith has tended to be founded on the unstable sands of theological conceptions and historical legends rather than on the solid rock of common-sense and experience and our Lord's common-sense gospel, which was based not on what anyone had thought or said or done, but on the common experience of mankind, which needs only to be put to the test to be proved.

Human nature being what it is, such teaching as that of

the gospel of our Lord has little chance of surviving as a potent influence in the world unless it is enshrined in some kind of religion; and a satisfactory religion must have a theology; but it should never be overlooked that it is the gospel that is the important thing. The theology and religious observances are no more than the frame to set off the gospel. All history has disclosed a dangerous tendency in such matters to exaggerate the importance of the frame and to overlook the masterpiece it contains. It is revealing sometimes to re-frame a picture; and the time would appear now to have come to wrap the traditional expressions of our religion and the traditional theology in metaphorical cellophane and lay them reverently aside in some sort of theological museum beside such conceptions as devil-possession, witchcraft, and the ancient Earth-bound astronomy on which much of the traditional theology, in common with astrology, is based; and to re-state the Christian faith in terms of the idiom and ways of thought, the language, of this present day and generation, using metaphors and symbols which have a real, vital, meaning in this present day, and which are suitable to commend and expound the gospel to present-day people.

This would not necessarily involve any violent breach with the traditional modes of religious expression of the past. All that is best in them could be retained, much as scientists do with their hypotheses and theories, discarding, revising, developing them when they are no longer adequate to aid in the understanding and exploration of the world as currently comprehended. It would only be doing more permanently, comprehensively, and authoritatively, what any effective preacher already does piecemeal from Sunday to Sunday.

The churches are much preoccupied with organisational unity; but what is of much more importance is what they are to unite for, what lead, what message, they are to give to the world and in what language—the language of two thousand years ago, or the language of today. There appears to be little chance of the churches holding the following they have, much less of winning the churchless millions, so long as they are handicapped by an out-moded theology and way of expression. As well try to wage war in this nuclear age with bows and arrows.

XV. Nicodemus

The originator of the Christian religion is not usually thought of as a philosopher; but his recorded sayings show a familiarity with the philosophical thought of his day. There is one passage in particular in the New Testament where his own philosophy seems to come to light—the story of his encounter with Nicodemus. It is immaterial for this purpose whether one regards that story as history or as just the framework for a theological exposition. The views propounded in the preceeding pages of this book seem to have much in common with the philosophy disclosed in that encounter.

To appreciate this one should understand that the expression 'son of man' which is used in that story is just the idiom for 'man', 'mankind', in the Aramaic language which Jesus spoke. There would appear to be little doubt, however, that the expression was used also on occasion as a sort of nickname for Jesus, even by himself. It seems to have carried some well understood associations and implications, such as those which appear, for instance, in the Dead Sea Scrolls. The result at this distance of time is that it is sometimes difficult to know whether, in any particular instance, the expression is used in the sense of 'man' or as a nick-name for Jesus. If in the story of this encounter the expression is interpreted as 'man', the whole incident becomes a philosophical dissertation; if on the other hand it is interpreted in the conventional way, as meaning simply 'Jesus', it becomes a religious one, embodying some of the central doctrines of the conventional Christian faith.

It is the philosophical interpretation, treating 'son of man' as meaning just 'man', that is experimented with in what follows. It is with some trepidation that this version is suggested, because the other interpretation, the religious and conventional one, is enshrined in phrases which have become dear to every Christian and hallowed by long usage; but the philosophical version also contains a message of supreme import; and there is some palliation in the fact that the particular doctrines embodied in the conventional religious interpretation do not depend solely on this passage, and would not necessarily suffer if this passage were read in a sense which entirely omits them.

It should also be appreciated that the expressions 'son of man' and 'son of God' appear to lend themselves to a certain amount of interplay in the Aramaic idiom.

Here then is an interpretation of the passage (John II, 23–III, 21) taking 'son of man' as meaning 'man'. It is a very free translation, perhaps more of a paraphrase than a translation, and it borrows from the Old Testament background to the discussion between Jesus and Nicodemus in order to elucidate the suggested meaning of the passage. It is primarily an impassioned assertion by Jesus of his faith in mankind and a stern rebuke to Nicodemus for not having the courage of his convictions.

The Story of Nicodemus

A few days after the incident at the wedding-feast at Cana of Galilee, the news of which had spread abroad, Jesus went up to Jerusalem for the feast of the passover; and while he was there people began to talk of him as a possible Messiah, because of the marvellous things he did. But Jesus was careful to be quite non-committal. He understood too well what men are like. No one could teach him anything on that score. And he did not want at that juncture to become involved in any movement of that sort.

One of these people was a man called Nicodemus, a well-known public figure, a pharisee, and a member of the ruling Council of the Jews. He sought Jesus out one night, under cover of darkness, to warn him of the danger in which he was putting everyone, under the very nose of the Roman Governor. He saluted Jesus with the flattering title of Rabbi (teacher).

'Rabbi,' he said, 'we have been talking about you; and we recognise that you must be a teacher inspired by God, because no one could do the wonderful things you do if God were not with him.'

'Yes, yes,' said Jesus, 'but a man cannot see the kingdom of heaven without being born again.'

'What?' said Nicodemus, taken aback. 'How do you mean "born again"? Do you mean to say a man can go back into his mother's womb and be born all over again?'

'It is quite simple,' said Jesus. 'Unless a man takes his life into his own hands and clears it of enslavement to animal instinct and re-shapes it according to the governance of the spirit he cannot enter into the Kingdom of Heaven. What is born of the body is just another body subject to physical laws and natural instincts. Only living spirit can give birth to spirit. There is no need to be so surprised because I said you must be born again. Spirit is something quite different from physical, material, body. It is not subject to the laws of nature but is as free as the winds, to come and go where it pleases and do what it likes. You can hear the sound of the wind but you cannot tell where it has come from or where it is going to. And so it is with living spirit; and you cannot hide its influence on a man's conduct and character. That is what a man is like whose spirit has come to birth.'

'But I do not follow that,' began Nicodemus.

'Do you mean to tell me,' replied Jesus, 'that you are a master of Israel and do not understand a simple thing like that? These are just matters of common knowledge and experience; and you question them. If you do not accept what I say when I speak of every-day experience, how will you accept it if I speak to you about the ultimate things—about the things of infinity and eternity? And, mark you, no one has gone up to heaven to discover such things for us. We have to depend for all our knowledge of them on man's own experience and thought and example. But then, you see, man himself comes from God. He was created by God in His own image, and the Kingdom of Heaven, joy without limit, is man's true destiny. God breathed the breath of life into man, and set eternity in his heart, so that he can never find rest till there is nothing more to achieve.

'So, just as Moses set up the brazen serpent in the desert, so that whenever anyone was bitten by a poisonous snake, if he believed in the saving power of the brazen serpent when he looked at it, he would live, so man must be held up for everyone to see, so that whoever believes in him should not be condemned to futility and failure but should enjoy life to the full—life of unlimited possibilities.

'You see, God liked this world He had created so much that He put the most articulate expression of Himself into it—man, created in the very image of God, after His own likeness. And He did not put man into the world for anything so futile as just to sit down and brood over life and weave theories about it and praise or condemn it, and then do nothing at all about it; but so that through him God's own work of creation might be carried on and the world developed and life enriched without limit.

'Anyone who believes in man is not condemned to such futility and failure; but anyone who does not believe in man is condemned already because he has not got faith in the fullest expression of God that man has been given.

'And this is how he is condemned. It is that God has given him the chance of a life of unlimited possibilities and has given him the intelligence to achieve it, and he has chosen instead a lower and unenlightened existence.

'People who follow that inferior way of life may be afraid of coming into the light in case it shows them up; but people who love enlightenment and progress stand for them openly, for everyone to see, so that men may recognise that these things are the workings of God.'

Nicodemus must have been stung by these last words and must have had much to think about as he made his way homewards that night. He was not wholly persuaded however to take an open stand for Jesus and what he stood for. Jesus on the other hand went on and gave his life for his faith in man. Nevertheless Nicodemus was so profoundly moved by his encounter with Jesus that he made bold to say a few words for him in his hour of crisis (John VII, 50–52) and to lay a tribute on his grave (John XIX, 39–42).

XVI. Death

Death poses the most difficult and commanding problem of all our philosophising. How can I say that my own existence is unquestionable when I know that sooner or later death will overtake me? The unquestionableness of my existence arises from the fact that it is I who am doing the thinking and that it is I who am conscious of all the affairs of my life; but when thought and consciousness are extinguished in death, what then? As we have noticed earlier more than once, nature (God) seems to have deliberately withheld from us any factual solution of this problem. There are straws at which we may grasp to indicate that there is some kind of survival for the human personality after bodily death; but they are pitifully inadequate to support any reasoned conclusion as to the permanence of survival.

And when we try to view the matter with the eye of faith there comes, to cloud the issue and bedevil our thoughts, the emotional stress of the death of someone near and dear to us; and the question does death end all assumes a new urgency.

In one sense the answer is plain. Like everything else that is, we are expressions of God; we are in some subtle way parts of Him. In Him we live and move and have our being. And so the stuff of which we are made can never cease to be. It came from God and to God it must return. And then too, as we ourselves have thus our lot and part in God, in universal existence, we can rest assured that our passionate desire for life, and for the lives of those we love, reflects an answering love and desire in the heart of the universe. And so, on either score, their and our continued existence in some form or other cannot be in doubt. It may be beyond our comprehension to envisage how God can shape our lives after the physical bodies which hitherto have given them form have disintegrated in death.* Our minds are not adapted to the under-

* Kant's 'practical postulate' of immortality, as part of his 'rational faith', apart from being only a hypothesis, takes us no further. It offers only the vaguest conception of what immortality might be.

standing of such mysteries. But we can confidently entrust ourselves and our loved ones to His keeping.

All this however leaves an element of vagueness. It leaves unsatisfied the passionate desire of our hearts for our loved ones who have passed over—our desire for them as we knew them, and for nothing but themselves. So it is comforting to reflect that we have within our own minds a guarantee that, whatever the forms and the ways and the means, God will preserve them, and not as mere abstractions but as living personalities, as the living souls we loved. Memory is the guarantee. Memory could not exist as a function of our being were it not a function of universal being, reflected, expressed, in us. Since we remember our loved ones, so must God.

Consider what that implies. The mind is a unity. Even with us there is no real division between the various functions of thought. There is something of all in each. No doubt in our restricted state of being there is a vital difference between the actual thing and the mere memory of it. But with Universal Being it is another matter. There can be no fundamental difference between the two things there—more than, for instance, between different states or spheres of existence. When it is God who does the remembering it must be, for that which He remembers, the same as existing, the same as living, the same as being created anew; because it is in God's 'mind' alone that we do exist. We are but thoughts—beloved thoughts—in the mind of God. So the ancient imagery of a resting place, a heaven, where our dear departed dwell with God is good enough to express what must in fact be a reality. It represents something which is as near to the truth as our minds can get.

Doubtless it may well be that a man might so conduct himself that Universal Existence might regret having brought him into being, and might banish him from memory—whatever the effect of that might be—something quite beyond our powers of comprehension. But even if that were so, our loved ones possess some lovable quality, else we could not love them; and for that quality, if for none other, God must love and cherish and remember them.

So these cherished memories of our loved ones are God's own pledge that we will meet again, changed maybe (for a living being can never remain entirely the same, whether in this life or any other) and in some state of being perhaps which we cannot at present envisage, yet the very ones whom we knew and loved. And not only so, but here and now, just as our love reaches out to them, their love must reach out to us, seeking to cherish and help and encourage us.

If our minds cannot envisage a life beyond the grave it cannot be because there is none. Universal Existence cannot cease to be; and we have our lot and part in it. It can only be because our ideas about immortality and ultimate reality are inadequate.

XVII. Other States of Existence

At the outset (Chap. II) reference was made to the circumstance that we have to peril our knowledge of the world outside ourselves on the validity of our logic—the validity of our processes of reasoning—by which, consciously or subconsciously, we deduce all our knowledge of the outside world. Let us pursue this matter a little further.

Our rules of logic are not something fundamental like the fact of existence, the fact that 'I am'. They are not something self-existing and absolute, something we discover and must just accept. They are largely if not entirely a thing of our own —of man's own—creating, a framework of abstract reasoning which the human mind has itself devised or developed for its own purposes. But, like pure mathematics, it would only be of academic interest if its propositions were not sufficiently aligned to the facts of experience and observation to make it useful in systematising our thoughts about these facts. A theory in pure mathematics may remain for long stored away in some scientific journal or library, forgotten and serving no useful purpose. And then some research worker comes upon a practical problem which fits its formulae, and the theory is brought into use and becomes part of practical applied mathematics. And so it is with logic. If its abstract propositions did not so closely fit the facts of observation and experience in the actual world in which we live as to give practical help in our reasoning about them, they would remain largely just academic curiosities soon forgotten by the world at large.

And so, whether or not it is strictly accurate to do so, it is a convenient short-cut to ascribe to the world the qualities of logic—to speak of them as if they were inherent in the world in which we live. It saves much circumlocution and side-steps a controversial subject, and it is justified by the fact that the world does possess qualities which are so well paralleled by the logical system. Thus it is common to speak of the geometry of a physical system (geometry being one form of logic), ascribing geometrical qualities to it whether or not in reality the geometrical qualities are only something in our own minds. We will adopt this mode of speech in what follows, for the sake of brevity; but it should not be overlooked that on one view it is only a figure of speech.

While our system of logic so well fits the actual world in which we live, there may be other states of existence for which an appropriate system of logic would be quite different from ours. That indeed may be a cause of difficulty for beings in one state of existence holding intelligent converse with beings in another. There is in principle no reason why the rules of logic and the laws which control the facts of life should be the same in one state of existence as in another.

This may be illustrated from mathematics, one of the purest forms of logic. The geometry of our ordinary world of observation can be validly expressed by Euclidian geometry; or, to express it otherwise, the world as we see it conforms to Euclidian geometry. It has three dimensions. A single straight line gives one dimension (length). Add another line, or others, at right angles, and thus make a plane or square, and you get a second dimension (breadth). Add another or others at right angles to both, and thus make a cube, and you get a third dimension (height). And so you have all the dimensions of the solid geometry of the world as we see it, which conforms to all the laws of Euclid's geometry. But any number of other dimensions may be added without destroying the mathematical validity of the resulting geometry. This constitues multi-dimensional geometry. For instance, take this square:

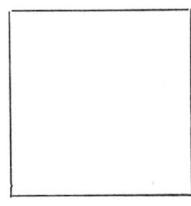

It is in two dimensions (length and breadth) and it conforms to all the propositions of Euclid's plane or two-dimensional geometry—so long as you keep the page flat. But bend the page; curl it round. Euclidian two-dimensional geometry then no longer applies to it, apart from the page. This is clear if you imagine the page away and the lines to be made of fine wire. You can see now that the figure no longer lies in a two-dimensional plane; and yet even if you add the third Euclidian dimension (height) to embrace it, this does nothing to help the figure to conform to the Euclidian propositions about squares and straight lines and angles. But leave the page in, or put it back in, and regard the figure as being a square on a flat plane, in spite of the actual curvature of the page, and all the propositions of Euclidian plane two-dimensional geometry apply to it notwithstanding that it no longer lies in a plane or within two dimensions. The curvature of the page has added a new dimension. It is now plane geometry in three dimensions instead of the Euclidian two. Or, to put it another way, the supplying of the page to fill in the interstices of your wire figure has furnished a new dimension which enables you validly to express all the geometrical properties of your (wire) square in terms of two-dimensional plane geometry. A Mercator's projection map is a typical instance of this.

It is to be observed however in passing that there is a limit to the validity of some of the transformations of this kind. A Mercator's projection map for instance becomes more and more distorted the nearer it approaches to the poles, until when it actually reaches a pole it breaks down completely and loses all validity. The pole, which in fact is a mere imaginary point without dimensions, becomes drawn out to a straight line the same length as the equator; and beyond that line the Earth's surface ceases altogether and there is nothing—a void. This does not correspond with anything in actuality. And there is a similar limit to the validity of many others of these transformations, each according to its own peculiar features. It is in such cases that the geometry is properly called non-Euclidian, although the term is also loosely applied to multi-dimensional geometry in general.

Now it will readily be seen that if, instead of a sheet of paper with a square drawn on it, you had a sheet of rubber the thickness of one side of the square, with the square forming part of its substance through and through so that it was now a solid cube, something like a piece of the pattern in a bit of inlaid linoleum, you would get the same effects and the same results by curling up the sheet of rubber; only now it would be three-dimensional solid geometry you were dealing with. And the curvature of the sheet of rubber would introduce a new, a fourth, dimension in addition to the three dimensions of Euclidian geometry. Allowing for that additional factor (the curvature of the sheet) all the propositions of Euclidian geometry would still hold for your cube; but without that factor they would not be valid when the sheet was bent. The cube would be all contorted.

You will observe that it is the precise amount and form of the curvature of the page or of the sheet which determines this new factor or dimension. The slightest variation of the curvature of the sheet would constitute a different factor—a different dimension. The cube would be differently contorted; and the possibilities of the amount of variation of the curvature and of the shapes into which you twist or fold your page or sheet are virtually unlimited, including such things as a constant change of the curvature if you introduce time as still another dimension. Indeed the flatness of the sheet (Euclidian geometry) is seen to be only one case, one particular instance, of all the possible variations of dimension which could be achieved by this method.

This is only one instance of a fourth dimension. Without going into details, the resources of pure mathematics provide infinite possibilities of multi-dimensional and non-Euclidian dimensions in geometry; and the scope of variation in each instance is infinite too, as in the case we have just been considering; nor can they always be visualised, as in this one. Non-Euclidian multi-dimensional geometry is a thing of wonderful beauty. It is like the music or the poetry of science. But the point which it is sought to make here is that it opens up a vista of an unlimited number of different possible states of existence from that in which we live, in each of which a different fourth dimension is introduced, so that the rules of our logic would not be valid in geometrical matters in these states nor the rules of logic in any of them be valid in any other; and yet in all of them, to a being living in them, the rules of logic might seem to be just what they seem to us, and their geometry might seem to be as Euclidian as ours seems to us.

They and their world might be made so. Their curved lines might seem to them to be straight, and our straight lines to be curved. We have in fact no means of knowing that our 'straight' lines are straight in ultimate reality (if indeed 'straightness' has any real meaning at all in ultimate reality). Indeed on the assumption that there is in ultimate reality no absolute system of geometry, the differences between such states of existence, including our own, would be purely relative. Any one of them might be taken with equal validity as being the one in which 'straight' lines are really straight.

And in all this we are dealing with one ingredient only in the make-up of worlds to live in—their geometrical form. The other ingredients of life, even in this world, are well-nigh infinite. The creator of them all could vary each of them, could subtract some and add others, unknown to us, and change their inter-relations, ad infinitum; and each change could be the basis of an entirely different world from that in which we live—could constitute a different state of existence.

Such states of course have nothing to do with any existence there may be entirely outside our scheme of existence, outside our universe. They would all be within our universe. They would each share some common denominator with all the others, including our own world.

Other beings may well live in such other states—in such other worlds. Perhaps our essential beings may go, when this life is over, to live in other worlds like that.

It is clear that the practical difficulties of establishing any communication between ourselves and beings in such other states of existence would be almost insuperable. It would be as though we were shut out from their world and had not the key to open the door, the common denominator, the right dimension, without which their lives, and hence their modes of thought and expression, would be unintelligible to us, without which we might be unable even to observe any sign of their existence, much as ether-waves pass unobserved till we have the key to tune in to them—a wireless receiving set suitably tuned.

That is one reason why it is doubtful whether we shall ever be able to hold articulate, intelligible, communion with those 'on the other side of the veil'. By all the laws of probabilities it is remotely unlikely that we should succeed in finding a common denominator for our different worlds. It is difficult even to believe that we could ever get over that difficulty in the case of inhabitants of the solar planets, if there are any or any who are sufficiently highly developed, who would at least be denizens of our own physical world—our own state of existence. The difficulty would probably be infinitely greater in the case of other states of existence altogether.

That however is not the main reason. One might be mistaken in all that. Scientific investigation has achieved so much it might after all even discover the key to intelligent communication with beings in another world. The main reason why we are unlikely to achieve it on any worth-while scale is that nature (God) seems so very obviously to have deliberately and intentionally shut us off from articulate, intelligible, converse with realms outside our own. This does not overlook the conversations which some people believe they hold with those who have 'passed over'; but, apart from a brief period immediately after bodily death, in all but a handful of authenticated cases these phenomena are explicable by other well-known psychic phenomena, such as telepathy; and the others are too few in number and too scanty in content to justify any conclusions in a field of knowledge of which we know so little. They would need to be multiplied a hundredfold. And the investigation is fraught with so many dangers to mental and spiritual stability that it should be engaged in only by experts.

XVIII. Conclusion

The main conclusions of this book have been reached by what was regarded as pure reasoning. Starting from the undeniable fact that 'I am', that I exist, that anyone exists, it has been sought to show that certain conclusions follow logically by deduction from that premiss. But in all this there lurks a paradox; because the whole edifice of thought thus built up is based on reason; and we have no guarantee that in ultimate reality the workings of our minds, the rules of our logic, are valid. In the last resort we must rely on faith for that. Indeed, if the scheme of thought developed in these pages is sound, the system of logic which serves our needs in this world is only one of an infinite variety of possible systems, each different, and each equally valid. The validity, the appositeness, of each would be relative to the particular state of existence to which it applied. Indeed the very existence of reason itself is but one of an infinity of possibilities. Reason just happens to be one of the ingredients of our particular form of existence; and it has grown and developed because it serves our ends in it.

So that when we get down to bed-rock realities the only thing on which we can stake everything is neither reason, nor belief, nor intuition, nor hope, nor aspiration, nor the urge to live, but is compounded of all these things and an infinity besides. It springs from the very core and essence of our beings. It is the thing we call faith.

What then? Is all our philosophising mere vanity and vexation of spirit? Far from it. Our philosophising may indeed show that within universal existence there are limits beyond which the human mind can find no bearings; but within these limits, where we can find bearings, reason is of fundamental importance.

Reason is what enables us to bring the material at our disposal, the world we live in, within the ambit of our wills, and so to express ourselves through it; and that is the aim and end of our being—to achieve joy by so doing. It is true we have no means of knowing how far the way the world appears to us is real, how far it gives a true picture of the realities behind the appearances, or how far it is permanent, whether it will continue to exist for even one moment beyond the present, or how far our ways or reasoning about it are valid, how far they hold in the world of ultimate reality. But here and now the world as we know it is very real to us, and it seems very permanent. It has existed for countless ages. And our logic has been proved over the same vast stretches of time to be validly applicable to it. So in these circumstances the only way to achieve anything in the world, the only way we can use such a situation to further our ends, is to act as though it were all that it appears to be and as though there were no question as to the validity or applicability of our logic. And our inner self, our faith, approves and urges us so to act. In other words, in all the affairs of this present life and this present world we live by faith, faith so sure and unquestioning that we are normally not even aware that it is an act of faith at all. And in that way reason is able to turn our world to our own uses and win more and more of it for our use.

And the same method can be applied to the world of ultimate reality, the reality behind the appearance of things. We have a constant and insatiable urge to know more and more of it so that we can bring more and more of it to our own uses. We want to use it to enlarge our horizons. We want to feel assured by our acquaintance with it that our life here is not all, that it is part of some vaster project that invests our little life here with dignity and meaning and makes it worth while; and we want to be assured that it is all something we can rely upon. The only thing to do in such circumstances is to use the rules of reason that we know, the logic that has proved valid in the world we live in, and carry it as far as we can into the world of the unknown beyond the appearance of things. And again our inner self, our faith, approves and urges us to do so. We use reason thus, in an act of faith, to get some bearings in the sphere of ultimate reality, much as we use imaginary lines of latitude and longitude to get bearings in geography and astronomy. In this way reason gains for us some glimpses of the realities beyond the world of sense and experience.

Primarily what we so learn is that we ourselves and all

we know and experience in this world, including its logic, are reflections however faint of something that exists in the infinity and eternity beyond. And so the act of faith is itself also a reflection of something in ultimate reality; and we are thus doubly justified. We are justified both by the urge itself, that is by faith, and by the knowledge that the urge, that our faith, has its origins in ultimate reality. So however much it needs faith to rely on reason, either in mundane affairs or in the things of ultimate reality, it is reason that gives content and meaning to our faith, it is reason that enlarges our understanding and so enlarges the scope of our living (though we must be careful not to press the method beyond the limits which reason itself imposes.) This is the very antithesis of Zen, the Japanese philosophy, which deprecates all preoccupation with such ultimate problems, as hindering the real business of life, which is to live.

The essence of the conclusions thus reached in this book is that all existence is an indivisible unity, and that we are all integral parts of it. Our separatenesses, our individualities, are only relative. So each of us has a vital interest in the success and happiness of the whole and of every part of it.

And so the supreme rule of the universe is love. On the one hand there is the love which the whole (God) bears for each part of it, including each of us. On the other hand there is the love which each part of the universe, including each one of us, bears for the whole (God) as He has expressed Himself in everything He has created; and that includes mankind. And, for us, mankind must always be the most important part of what He has created.

THE END